I0816093

WHY ALANIS MORISSETTE MATTERS

Evelyn McDonnell
Series Editor

BOOKS IN THE SERIES

Andrew Chan, *Why Mariah Carey Matters*
Lynnée Denise, *Why Willie Mae Thornton Matters*
Allyson McCabe, *Why Sinéad O'Connor Matters*
Steacy Easton, *Why Tammy Wynette Matters*
Caryn Rose, *Why Patti Smith Matters*
Tanya Pearson, *Why Marianne Faithfull Matters*
Charles L. Hughes, *Why Bushwick Bill Matters*
Stephanie Phillips, *Why Solange Matters*
Adele Bertei, *Why Labelle Matters*
Fred Goodman, *Why Lhasa de Sela Matters*
Karen Tongson, *Why Karen Carpenter Matters*
Tom Smucker, *Why the Beach Boys Matter*
Donna Gaines, *Why the Ramones Matter*

WHY ALANIS MORISSETTE MATTERS

Megan Volpert

UNIVERSITY OF TEXAS PRESS
AUSTIN

Printed in the United States of America
First edition, 2025

♾ The paper used in this book meets the minimum requirements of ANSI/NISO Z39.48-1992 (R1997) (Permanence of Paper).

Library of Congress Cataloging-in-Publication Data

Names: Volpert, Megan A., author.
Title: Why Alanis Morissette matters / Megan Volpert.
Other titles: Music matters.
Description: First edition. | Austin : University of Texas Press, 2025. | Series: Music matters | Includes bibliographical references.
Identifiers: LCCN 2024017612
ISBN 978-1-4773-3087-6 (hardcover)
ISBN 978-1-4773-3088-3 (pdf)
ISBN 978-1-4773-3089-0 (epub)
Subjects: LCSH: Morissette, Alanis. Jagged little pill (Album) | Morissette, Alanis—Criticism and interpretation. | Alternative rock music—History and criticism.
Classification: LCC ML420.M6185 V65 2025 | DDC 782.42166092—dc23/eng/20240521
LC record available at https://lccn.loc.gov/2024017612

doi:10.7560/330876

CONTENTS

INTRODUCTION

Oh hello Mr. Man
You didn't think I'd come back
You didn't think I'd show up with my army
And this ammunition on my back

ALANIS MORISSETTE, "Right Through You"

These four lines have been on the top of my epigraph list since I was in high school—I just didn't know they would appear at the front of a book that is actually about Alanis Morissette herself. For many of us who slouched against the chain-link fence with the Class of '99 banner drooping from it, hovering like ornery ghosts within the thin zone between Gen X and Millennialism, Alanis is the conduit through which we still cry out loud.

On the weekend of my fourteenth birthday, *Jagged Little Pill* reached the top spot on the Billboard 200. It stayed in the top ten for an unprecedented seventy-two weeks and, thanks to the constant scream of it on the radio and on MTV, it started to seem to me that my coven was powerful enough to survive high school. I listened to *JLP* on loop on my yellow Sony Sport Walkman on a cassette that I begged someone to make for me. Despite being a queer with young, deadbeat parents and suffering heavily from that chronic condition known the world over as generalized teenage femaleness, whatever kind of hooligan I was, I wasn't snatching albums off the racks at the Tower Records at the mall.

"Right Through You" spoke to me, as a fledgling writer, the most because it presented information about what to expect when attempting to deploy creativity in a marketplace. There would be assholes. I was already cynical about most adults, especially business-minded ones with any real money, so Alanis provided confirmation for my intuition about the situation. It felt really nice to know somebody could see me. Alanis prepared me, though she was barely twenty-one when *JLP* came out and probably felt very ill-prepared herself. She gave me the power to stand in my rage and to use my anger as an energy to do good in the world. I say "Alanis" not because we're friends—although parasocially speaking, I am certainly her friend—but because no academic treatment of Madonna ever refers to her as Ciccone. It's a useless form of rigor and it verges on insolence when the one-name celebrity is female. Let Alanis be a queen.

Her epic war against Mr. Man, begun when both of us were teenagers, still appeals. She is our raging sage. She is our punk monk. As a result of this aggressively female noise, I did make it out of high school alive—and then realized I was tough enough to return to the scene of the crime as a tenth-grade English teacher at a public high school in the north 'burbs of a major metro area not unlike the one I grew up in. People ask me how I do it: how I relate to the secret hearts of those on this planet who are simply reaching for a fifteenth year that doesn't suck too much. My army is over three thousand strong now, full of legendary children. When they have shown me Lana Del Rey or Billie Eilish or Olivia Rodrigo, I have shown them Alanis.

Something inside of me is frozen there, at fourteen-going-on-forty. And whatever that thing is, it's got Alanis on repeat because there is the laugh of Medusa in it. There are qualities in the lyrics and vocals, in the videos and her subsequent work in other genres of page and stage, that capture the ineffable psychology of specifically female existential awareness. *JLP* is a manual and a manifesto. Alanis is not on the model of a radical feminist assassin or separatist. Instead, she offers the sound of Antigone knocking at Creon's gate. Her ongoing body of work, with *JLP* at its center, is a prime example of what French feminists in the seventies called *écriture feminine*. Women's writing. Women writing their way out of oppression by using words and forms that escape classic (cough patriarchal cough) approaches to writing.

Of course, in not bowing down to conventionalist rock expectations, Alanis paradoxically made oh so much money while simultaneously receiving at best mixed reviews and definitely not enough awards. *JLP* is one of only three albums to sell above fifteen million copies in the US since Nielsen Soundscan began tracking such stats in 1991. Alanis is nipping at the heels of fellow Canadian Shania Twain, and then she only needs to sell a million further copies to overtake Metallica. Yet she's been denied Rock and Roll Hall of Fame induction since 2016. Hell, Carole King didn't get in as a performer until I was thirty-nine, even though she'd been eligible since I was fourteen and even though my mom probably feels about *Tapestry* just as I do about *JLP*. On the *Rolling Stone* revised 2020 list of the top 500 albums of all time, *JLP* was slotted—isn't it ironic?—at 69. They gave her three sentences.

Any substantive discussion of her legacy has been so far barred by the keepers of the canonical gates. Admittedly, my own fandom of Alanis has not gone the distance in banging on those gates. My senior year of high school, I dismissed most of *Supposed Former Infatuation Junkie* because my own angst was still growing and I didn't want to hear any of hers receding. The *Alanis Unplugged* album pushed me further away because my juvenile Alanismania couldn't cope with all the vocal variations she layered onto her classic lyrics. I was pissed off that she prevented me from credibly singing along, which I now see clearly as one of the superior powers of her poetry, the way it's able to be sung through the lens of so many genre twists and communicate effectively yet slightly differently in each of them. Her feminist strategies were more advanced than mine, a ghost of future revolution. By 2002, *Under Rug Swept* felt like a joke about her being relegated to the dustbin.

So I went to college and forgot about my love of Alanis. We went our separate ways, both seeming happier or at least very much wiser now in middle age. During my period of inattentiveness, her world of course did not stop turning. Like many people, I checked back in thanks to a nudge from the announcement that *JLP* was being turned into a Broadway show. To my delight but not my surprise, I feel much more able now to appreciate the full spectrum of her work rather than just harkening back to *JLP* for a few weeks and then forgetting about it again. This time I dove right for the rabbit hole, digging deeper into all the albums I'd missed during my twenties and thirties and moreover into the fascinating array of other projects through which Alanis continues to communicate with unrivaled clarity, wit, and urgency. Neither of us has mellowed with age. As it turns out, all these little green shoots that for twenty years I'd brushed off as nothing like the sturdy, six-foot sunflower of *JLP* are rhizomatic, full of ideas and missions just below the surface that are solidly linked to all the things I loved about *JLP*. The seedling of that album has grown into an undeniably lush garden.

This book is meant to convince you to take a look at what Alanis has accomplished since her debut album, to appreciate both how her work has evolved and how facets of her subsequent projects are coated in a thin layer of 1995. She never dropped the banner we carried along with her during that time. She stitched more pieces onto it, patched it up as needed, and got older and wiser about how to wave it. Alanis is still at work, still doesn't oblige any "wine and dine." She continues to see, feel, know, and walk right though that bullshit. If we are not overly careful, women-identified people face a lifetime of erasures, perpetually viewed as nothing more than meal tickets or sweet, backloaded puppets. And yet Alanis compels us to have faith that if we have the courage to give voice to whatever is the feminist equivalent of Whitman's barbaric yawp, Mr. Man will inevitably be forced to wonder why his name doesn't appear in our credits. It's a way of speaking truth to power—to parents, priests, and pricks—and it does take an army, in which I am proudly one member. May this little book serve as part of our ammunition.

1

THE SILENCE THAT PETRIFIES

Children were supposed to be seldom seen and never heard in the house where I was raised. So I went upstairs to my attic bedroom, feeling the heat rise but trying to keep my nose in a book until I was seventeen and could escape to college. It didn't work. My father called me "smart mouth," and sometimes he said it with pride to my uncles at bowling league but mostly he yelled it at full volume right at my face while he was putting a bar of soap in my mouth. Usually Dial. The girls got soap and the boys got the belt. I don't really know what my mother got but she stayed with him until I was in my twenties anyway.

Throughout my four decades on this planet, it has remained obvious to me that men generally want women to shut up. Let's pick men apart because I can't help it. They are dumb to want this, because women of course have so much to contribute to the world. Even more narrowly and selfishly, they are petrified that silence is actually the sound of women plotting, gathering strength, prepping the revolution. Any time I got excellently deep into a book, my father would holler from the den two flights down and I'd have to come running immediately. His investigation always began the same way: you've been quiet a long time; what're you up to up there?

It was a nightmare for my music needs. Couldn't blast

Alanis in my headphones because god forbid it should drown out my father so well that he would feel compelled to get out of his La-Z-Boy, and couldn't blast her on the boombox because he would fling that retrospective ultimatum about turning it off because I wouldn't turn it down. He once made me toss my copy of *In Utero* because he said it was druggie music. I didn't want to know what he thought of Alanis. All I really wanted was some peace, man. Or else I wanted to hunt the hunter.

At fifteen, I was a subject matter expert in the jagged little pill. Then thirty years of burying all the bodies went by and I'm here now, trust-falling backward into my teenage wasteland in order to say that Alanis matters because she continues to help millions of people get through life for a while. This book is not a straightforward biographical treatment, though relevant factoids and trivia nuggets shall be revealed in due course. We are going to meet one of our feminist makers and should expect to be humbled by her humble nature. Given that Alanis too has gotten older, we can trace the sturdy fort she's been building atop the foundational ideas from *Jagged Little Pill*. Your expectation for what kind of book this is should proceed directly from that image of the mad grrrl in the attic, reading heavy philosophy and psychology books while Alanis plays oh so softly in the background. I was up there examining her every off-kilter lilt in phrasing, parsing each of her lyrics with one finger stuck in the index of a textbook on existentialism.

So we begin, not with a standard-issue "Alanis was born in blah blah blah," but with that moment where the legend was first made: the opening track on the *JLP* album. "All I Really Want" mostly takes the form of a list poem articulating the things everybody wants in life. These include complicated qualities to sustain such as common ground, comfort, justice, and patience. It sucks to want things you can't have, so it's not a surprise that Alanis characterizes herself as all strung out from the loneliness of it. She can acknowledge the difficulty of accomplishing all she really wants while simultaneously mocking anyone who would put her down for being too intense. She knows she can stress you out, and yet beyond your weariness Alanis hears the sound of pretenses falling. She's annoyingly self-aware of how annoying she can be and happy to poke the listener with a confrontational demonstration of this tendency.

Eight stanzas in: here, can you handle this? She holds out four little beats of silence. No words and the music drops down to almost nothing. It's not even a total silence, but it's enough in that it performs how silence can be strategic and feminist. Thoughts that Alanis speculates about would naturally rush in to fill this tiny moment of silence: bills, your ex, deadlines, when you think you're going to die, and longing for the next distraction. None of those are happy thoughts. This is a combative silence, not a comfortable or merely awkward one. Poised against this onslaught of earthly obstacles that you can't handle are all these beautifully utopian flashes in her list of wants, which in the end boil down to one thing, a soulmate on her own wavelength who can catch the drift and share with her deeper intellectual intercourse.

It's a tall order and she knows it. That's why she is consumed by the chill of solitary. Alanis is not at all prone to using proper nouns in her lyrics, but in this song, she namechecks Estella. To offer Amelia Havisham's icy young protégé from *Great Expectations* as a point of identification is not that eccentric. The precarity of female life makes it seem as though we are all at risk of becoming the archetypal, bitter beggars found in every Dickens novel. After being jilted at the altar, Miss Havisham spends her whole life rotting away in a wedding dress while training Estella to break men's hearts and then deploying her to do so. Together they're very good at this endeavor, Havisham serving vengeance on the male half of the species as Estella reels them in and then spits them out. These two women have learned to be unloving. They are characterized as villains, albeit melancholy ones.

But all they really want is a way to get their hands untied—from marriage, from men, from the entire Victorian apparatus of repressive societal expectation. They're quite relatable, actually. Estella is a good frame of reference for girlhood as a commodification process. Despite the alleged privileges of her material wealth, objectification is always expensive in the soul department and it doesn't matter whether you come out of it as a virgin or a whore. This is enraging, and though they often stumble, at least these women Charles Dickens made up are white-hot in their efforts at deliverance, working that extremely potent magic known as turning the tables. Killing the killer is mighty tempting because it follows nicely from that old gem that the best defense is a good offense. Can't really blame these women, so might as well join them. Relating to Estella did not assist me or Alanis in establishing healthy sexual boundaries when we were young, to say the very least. And all of us in real life and in fiction keep getting asked why we are so angry.

There is no shortage of synonyms for rage, nearly all

with strongly negative connotations, and most of them have been applied to Alanis over the years. In November 1995, she appeared on the cover of *Rolling Stone* in a drapey white button-down shirt and minimalist black leggings, her hair tumbling softly around her shoulders as she smiles at the camera. Next to this cheery image, in giant black lettering the headline nevertheless reads "Angry White Female." Try searching "Alanis anger" or "Alanis angry" and watch the internet generate hundreds of links. As if anger is her wavelength. It isn't. This is a fundamental misinterpretation of her energy. And mine. We only figured it out later on, not when we were girls.

Alanis is a highly sensitive person. She helped make a documentary about this in 2015. *Sensitive* is an hour-long film about the psychological research of Dr. Elaine Aron, who published the bestseller *The Highly Sensitive Person* in 1996. High sensitivity is a personality trait: not a disorder but an innate survival strategy found equally in males and females in dozens of species, not only humans. About 20 percent of people possess these attributes and most of us become artists, healers, or supervillains. Nowhere on Alanis's Wikipedia page does it mention that she is an HSP, even though this is beyond a doubt one of the most foundational aspects of her self-concept and an ongoing area of exploration for her. Much like me in this book's intro, she's up there in the attic flipping through psych textbooks, too.

Dr. Aron uses the acronym DOES to distinguish the main features of a highly sensitive person. The D is for depth of processing. Spare us the Netflix queue with a thousand too many choices for us to get bogged down in because we despise the drudgery of searching for a needle in a haystack. HSPs use more of the parts of our brains that are devoted to deeper integration of knowledge. We tend to be very intuitive, to make decisions quickly, and to maintain a high level of awareness of our surroundings. After I was born, I was busy soaking up so much of the world that I uttered my first words very late—so late that my mother feared I might be deaf and had me tested for it. I'm one part Sherlock Holmes and one part canary in the coal mine. This is the reason why HSPs are often seen as good leaders, or as rock stars. We are relentless. We have no concept of time other than it is flying.

The O is for overstimulation. Due to our profoundly massive attention span, we can become stressed or burnt out more easily than other people. Too much stimulation can knock us to the floor. This is especially true in circumstances requiring a lot of social interaction or where our five senses encounter many things to be processed. Also spare us the schmoozy corporate meet-and-greet or the all-day field trip to an amusement park—unless we've planned for it well in advance, which we are very good at and eager to do. We like to check boxes on an itinerary and our list-making is legendary. For many years, I thought I might have Asperger's or some other high-functioning form of autism. Imagine all the possible challenges in going to a stadium rock and roll show, let alone the responsibility of being the main attraction on stage.

The E has two meanings: emotional reactivity and empathy. When looking at positive or negative pictures, the brains of HSPs light up with greater responsiveness in the areas associated with emotion. Because I didn't have the mostly good childhood that Alanis did, her big happy feelings while looking at positive pictures will be even bigger than mine. We are empaths because our mirror neurons are more active than average. This makes us fantastic imitators and also enables us to have a keen grasp of how others are feeling because we somewhat feel their feelings ourselves. When we look at pictures of unhappy people, our brains tell us not just to feel their unhappiness but also to do something to help. No doubt this was part of my motivation to return to high school as a teacher, a trusted adult who helps an audience of thirty-five teenagers every hour. HSPs are eager to help because we get such a strong hit of feeling from it. In the documentary, Alanis speaks of striving to be conscientious about absorbing the heightened emotionality of her fanbase and how she has begun to think of her audience as full of HSPs.

The S is for sensory processing sensitivity. We sense the subtle. I have a nose for perfume and Alanis has an ear for song. This is not due to any physically superior quality in our nose or ears, but rather to our tendency to notice minutiae that most other people miss. Our brains get more active than other people's do when we are confronted by the same stimuli. An HSP is not likely to know more words than a non-sensitive, but an HSP is far more likely to grasp the nuanced connotations of words or the tone of their deployment in conversation. That's part of why we make such great poets. It's also why we struggle with the heightened scrutiny of the spotlight and the kinds of criticism that come with notoriety. Spare us from celebrity.

In the *Sensitive* documentary, Alanis tells Dr. Aron that until she became aware of the concept of highly sensitive people, she simply felt crazy. She felt in some vague, nagging way that she was too weird and didn't belong even in her own pretty nice family. She sensed her giftedness as a curse, very much like Estella. All she really wanted was a way to calm the angry voice. But in reframing Alanis's work within the context of her temperament as a highly sensitive person and grasping how this is frequently at odds with prevailing patriarchal systems of value that are the corrupted ways of this land, we can begin to understand that she is not angry. She's biologically wired to be intense, and she's frustrated by your apathy.

2

TO REMIND YOU

Each track of *Jagged Little Pill* has its own cornucopia of literary and historical analogies and connections worth analyzing. The mission of "You Oughta Know" finds a firm parallel in the ancient Greek drama *Antigone*, by Sophocles. While the latter is about love of country and the former is about love of a person, they both invest heavily in the problem of what to do about Mr. Duplicity. Both stories focus on a teenage girl whose idealism is getting stomped on by a powerful older man who lied and cheated his way into an undeserved position. These are stories in which our heroine demands what she is due, politicking promises made in the past and continuing to hold open a memory space in which these obligations remain active.

In case you have not read the play, please allow this English teacher the indulgence of providing an overview. Antigone is a daughter of the famous Oedipus, who blinded himself upon learning he'd inadvertently married and fathered children with his own mother. In his exile after this discovery, Oedipus wandered with Antigone as his caretaker, so she received a world-class education through life experiences that were not at all common for young women in this time period. She'd been around the block and seen plenty of things by the time her father died, and she returned to Thebes. Meanwhile, back in Thebes, an enormous struggle for power had just concluded. Her two brothers had promised each other to switch off ruling the kingdom from year to year, but one brother broke his promise and refused to give up the throne. Out came the swords and the brothers succeeded in killing each other.

Into this power vacuum stepped our villain, their uncle Creon, an egotist who was only too happy to rule. His first decree was that one of the brothers would not get the honorable burial that Greek culture deemed essential for proper passage into the spirit realm. He set one of them up to look like a traitor when Creon himself was the real traitor. Antigone arrived home to Thebes and immediately set about unlawfully burying her allegedly disgraced brother, until Creon's guards carted her off to jail. Regardless of big arguments and ultimatums from Creon, Antigone stood firm in her request to give her brother a proper burial despite the consequence—which was that she would be sealed away in a cave until she died. The gods intervened to punish Creon in a number of ways, and he ran to the cave to free Antigone, but he was too late. She looked death in the face, taking her own life by hanging instead of waiting for starvation to creep its way in.

Creon gave one face to the world and another to Antigone. He publicly purported to be just the type of leader his city-state needed, but privately he was cruelly selfish and shortsighted. Antigone's knowing and willful breaking of the law concerning her brother's burial was a strategic method of petitioning Creon to privately live up to his public persona as a good guy looking to return Thebes to a state of spiritual health. I've taught this play to high school students maybe forty times, and every single time we deliberated over what would constitute a happy ending for this tale. This is the same line of inquiry sparked by "You Oughta Know." The two main characters do not end up peacefully coexisting. Our heroine remains dumped by her boyfriend, just as Antigone remains dead. But Creon is doomed now to live his life knowing he was in the wrong, knowing that his own hubris led to tragedy. Alanis seems to share this vision of a possible future in which the bad guy must simply admit he has been bad.

The speaker in the song is showing up to bug her ex in the middle of his shiny new life. All she wants is to remind him that the mess he made is still lurking in the background. Perhaps she could just forgive him and move on, but her ex made promises about sticking around forever that he clearly did not keep. Rather than feeling a responsibility to let those promises go, Alanis instead makes her case for keeping the memory of the failed promise alive. This is much like the agenda of Miss Havisham that we examined in chapter 1. The song creates a space where the injustice of the breakup remains on display, unfaded, the painfulness of it occasionally reanimated for both partners whenever she scratches her nails down someone else's back. She may have other partners and she may become less of a mess, yet she nevertheless persists in holding open the prospect of her ex's eventual accountability.

There is still a huge amount of real-life demand for this mystery ex to indeed be held accountable. All these many years she has refused to say who the song is about. The most common theory is that the culprit is Dave Coulier, comedian and *Full House* television "uncle." But letting the man's identity remain unknown keeps the focus on the central question, which is not whether any specific man was lousy to Alanis but how we mete out justice against the generic figure of Mr. Duplicity. She doesn't want to be subservient, or for her life plans or happiness to be at the mercy of a two-faced liar's whims. The tether of the song is supposed to tug at him as much as it tugs at her, and this symbolism would be significantly undercut if the vague persona were traded for a specific person.

Look at what happens every time Carly Simon teases another new detail about the identity of the man in "You're So Vain." Some filthy rich guy once paid $50,000 at auction for Simon to reveal who the song was about, on the condition that he keep it confidential. Every time she reveals one letter of the subject's name to the public, there is a brief media storm as people clamor over the possible celebrity suspects. So we rehash the myriad of prickish deeds done by Jagger or Bowie or Beatty or Cassidy, losing sight of the much more widespread problem of men who walk into parties like they're walking onto a yacht. This archetypal narcissist in his stupid apricot scarf owns everything in his line of sight—the girls, the jet, the horses. The fact that there are a dozen serious real-life contenders for Simon's character is worth a chuckle, lest we gag. She's said it's a composite of several men and of course it is.

The stories of these two songs and the story of *Antigone* are about how such men deploy their privilege to silence any opposition. Their fantasy is that they are free to forget what they have done, until the wreckage knocks on their door as the women in these stories do, traversing that fantasy and thus revealing it as less than true, as not entirely viable. Getting a visit from the ghosts of relationships past forces the men in the stories to at least briefly acknowledge their own precarity. These women are not letting the so-called winners of the break-ups be the only ones who get to write their shared history. A woman's refusal to let these wounds close up is a means of resistance to the patriarchal fantasy that men can get away with everything without paying any price for it. Alanis has this cross to bear, of being duped by Mr. Duplicity, and to try to deny her that cross would be adding another layer of injustice. She will write her own stories.

So far we have drawn a connection between politics and romance in the conflicts orbiting around a Mr. Duplicity character, in the common stories shared between one theatrical drama and some song lyrics. There are other equally symbolic parallels, or echoes, between the life and work of Alanis and the mythic constructs of Antigone. Both Antigone and Alanis were privileged to see many parts of the world. Alanis's father taught the children of Canadian soldiers overseas, so Alanis traveled around Europe every weekend between the ages of three and six, soaking up places like Holland, Austria, Germany, Yugoslavia, Greece, Switzerland, and France in her family's camper van.

As a matter of personality, when they were young both Antigone and Alanis were accustomed to being thought of as old souls, or children with a knowledge far beyond their physical years. Paul Cantin, the Canadian journalist who was the first to publish a biography of Alanis way back in 1997, noted that when her giftedness and determination to succeed began to lose her friends at school, Alanis mostly shook it off as something she couldn't do anything about, wondering why anyone would ask her to be less than her fully realized self. She and Antigone share a similar attitude toward anyone who would ask them to dumb down their thinking or behave somewhat more normatively and quietly. Beginning at age nine, Alanis wrote poems with the intention of making them into songs. Just as Antigone rolled up her own sleeves when she saw no one was brave enough to defy Creon and bury the neglected brother, Alanis had to self-produce her first album at the age of fourteen when there was no interest from major labels.

Even her biggest fans sometimes forget that Alanis released two Canada-only albums with MCA Records Canada before Maverick Records put out *Jagged Little Pill* in 1995. The 1991 debut, *Alanis*, scored her three singles in the Canadian Top 40 plus a Juno Award for Most Promising Female Vocalist of the Year. Her 1992 album, *Now Is the Time*, produced three more Top 40 hits but sold fewer than half the number of copies of its predecessor. Songs for both albums were cowritten with producer Leslie Howe, who had had some success with his own late eighties dance pop duo, One to One. If the mentor one collaborates with in the creative work of writing an album has expertise in dance pop, the album that comes out of the collaboration is likely to tend toward dance pop.

The other mentor in Alanis's professional life was Stephan Klovan, whose ice-skating career had shaped his style of management. Based on Klovan's advice, Alanis trained to repress any stress or anxiety while performing, to keep smiling no matter what. The performance and its reliability were the main thing, not honesty or vulnerability. Klovan got her so many gigs singing the national anthem, "O Canada," for political and athletic events that she became known as the Anthem Girl. When he sent her to compete on *Star Search* and she lost, she was told to focus on the fact that she got to be on a nationally syndicated television show. Klovan thought the key was simply exposure, regardless of winning or losing. Alanis had to put her faith in the wisdom of those who had more experience on this path than she did, but surely it is a struggle for any teenager to lean on adults for advice and then discover that their best-laid plans can still fail.

Disputes between Klovan and Howe centered on what strategy was best to rocket Alanis to the top of the music business. Klovan wanted to invest heavily in time on stage, getting as much performance visibility as possible, while Howe thought making a killer album in the studio was the ticket to stardom. Alanis was a mere fourteen years old, so Klovan and Howe both fell under the assumption that her destiny was in pop music, making the kinds of records other fourteen-year-old girls would enjoy listening to. Although she bristled at being referred to as Canada's answer to Tiffany or Debbie Gibson, Alanis might have leapt for joy at any comparison to Olivia Newton-John. The first time Alanis ever saw the movie *Grease*, she was instantly obsessed with the role of Sandy and would act out literally the entire story, of course with all the songs, for her family at home. This was when she was only four years old. According to Cantin's biography, when her family later visited Hollywood, Alanis marched up to Newton-John's home in Malibu, hit the buzzer, and spoke into the intercom just to vow that she would one day be as big as her hero. Are you there, Olivia? It's me, Alanis.

Of course, Alanis did not subsequently become big as a dance queen. She transformed into an alternative rocker. Her detractors have sometimes argued that the voice of *Jagged Little Pill* is just another commercialized persona, accusing Alanis of manufacturing this more lucrative identity on the heels of her failure to adequately play the role of pop starlet. But if this were the case, from our historical viewpoint we can pronounce it an admirably long con given how she has stuck with her alt vibe for so many decades. I've always seen the change as akin to Sandy's transformation in *Grease*, wherein the heroine steps into some big hair and leather pants, dangles a cigarette, and compels Danny to get back together with her because that's what she wants him to do.

These aren't superficial changes Sandy has made, despite them being contrary to her image throughout most of the movie. The point is that Sandy chose a new path that was more aligned with her values. And here's a fun alignment that can hardly be accidental: *JLP* was released on June 13—the same release date as *Grease*. Perhaps like Sandy, Alanis was tired of being seen as the good girl all the time. Just as when Antigone's final drastic act of suicide shocked Creon into learning his lesson, Sandy's transformation forced Danny to right his previous wrong, publicly declaring his true affection for her despite having snubbed her at school all year after their loving summer. The stories of Antigone and Sandy and Alanis are of a piece. They harmonize.

Show business houses an abundance of people who might be sorted into the Mr. Duplicity archetype. It's tempting to launch into a long sidebar about Newton-John's costar, John Travolta, and examine the influence of his membership in the Church of Scientology on his career at that time. But then we may stray from the metaphorical territories of totalitarianism into literal ones. Here's a quick literal one: Alanis's mother came to Canada when she was ten years old because her family wanted to escape the turmoil of the failed Hungarian Revolution of 1956.

A less alarming but equally literal example might be the very popular Canadian sketch comedy series for preteens, *You Can't Do That on Television*, which simultaneously aired in the US on the paid cable television station Nickelodeon. When she was in junior high in 1986, Alanis appeared on five episodes and was forbidden during this window of time from cutting her hair or otherwise altering her appearance for the sake of preserving continuity for the viewers. She left quickly because it was evident that she was too much of a grown-up. She didn't laugh at fart jokes like the other child actors did, and she read books during the breaks from filming.

The show had a running gag from the very first episode, which was simply to drop a pile of green goo on the head of any character who said the phrase "I don't know." This sliming was so representative of the show that eventually it became the visual trademark of the entire Nickelodeon brand. During her brief stint on the series, Alanis was slimed three times, but only one of those scenes was aired. The slime mixture itself was disgusting and actors largely hated whenever it was their turn to be subjected to it, yet the slime couldn't be avoided. The fact that it wasn't a surprise did not make it any less traumatic. As a result, probably many of the show's endless parade of young people grew up into adults that have strongly negative associations with the phrase "I don't know." It's a dismissive phrase, one that sweeps things under the rug. It's the phrase Mr. Duplicity will use to keep insistent questioning at bay. When I hear Alanis singing to him, lobbing the litany at him about whether his new lover speaks eloquently or whether she would have his baby, I assume he is just running in the other direction and screaming, "I don't know!" I like to think in "You Oughta Know" Alanis is basically sliming her ex. It is the green goo, the mess he made, reminding him that she will not be ignored.

3

FOR YOUR OWN DAMN GOOD

Children are meant to evolve beyond their parents. Each fresh generation is supposed to have it somewhat better than their living ancestors did when they were younger. Perhaps this is why it feels so normal for most teens to despise their parents. Those feelings are part of the growing pains needed to surpass the oldsters. The negativity that young people feel toward their elders is a way of stepping on the gas pedal and blazing past the past into the future of their dreams. Alanis had, by all accounts, a happy childhood with supportive parents, even if any household trying to navigate stardom on behalf of one of its kids is going to have its share of obvious challenges and insidious pitfalls. It would be easy to assume a song like "Perfect" is a parody of parental psychology and that Alanis hated her guardians just as much as the rest of us hated ours.

A deeper reading must acknowledge that there are no actual parents in the song and that what we have instead is a very fine rhetorical example of the many perspectives that produce a paternalistic attitude. The song could also be understood as criticizing Alanis's own ambitious standards for herself, examining her internal drive for perfectionism as something easily conflated with traditional paternalism. There's a mean little workhorse inside of Alanis that is constantly reminding her to win, to keep smiling, to try harder—as if by her perfection Alanis protects her own pride and ensures her redemption for whatever she screwed up before.

And the nerve of that song's speaker, suggesting that all this pressure being applied is "for your own damn good." The result is that "Perfect" asks to what extent we are aware of what should constitute our own good. When we act paternalistically toward ourselves in the way that the song evokes, when we parent ourselves from a competitive place that assumes one very hard-charging and narrow pathway to success, as so many of us have done, it's an act of self-hatred.

Dick Schwartz's research on Internal Family Systems (IFS) argues that the self is made up of many parts, and these parts ought to be in conversation with each other so that all parts can be validated as gifts that manage or protect a person in different, wise ways. He teaches self-compassion as the road to empathy for others. If we stop viewing our lives as one monolithic narrative, then we can begin to stop imposing such flat representations upon our view of others, too. This psychological mindset shift can assist in trauma recovery, addiction therapy, and depression treatment. Alanis sought out Schwartz as she was going through her second bout of postpartum depression while simultaneously running herself ragged, as usual, on the hamster wheel of work addiction.

In her foreword to Schwartz's 2021 book, *No Bad Parts: Healing Trauma and Restoring Wholeness with the Internal Family Systems Model*, Alanis identifies a number of her own parts: angry, mother, artist, financially responsible, financially irresponsible, free spirit, murderous rage, shame, terrors, depression, aches, yearnings, humiliations, grief, generous, intelligent, leadership, gifted, sensitive, empathic. She wrote that the result of using IFS to integrate all these parts within her higher self was that she could "begin to feel the agendaless-ness" of what Schwartz calls the eight C's: creativity, courage, curiosity, connection, compassion, clarity, calm, and confidence. These are the things that rise up and come through when you are just being the way you are.

By contrast, the speaker in "Perfect" has no access to any feeling of agendaless-ness. The songwriter counters the heavy agenda of her inner totalitarian by performatively meditating on the flow of time in consideration of the good. While the song's speaker never lives in the moment, instead firing off demands about the future to remedy the past, the songwriter herself constructed that list of demands in under twenty minutes, in more or less a single take, for a stream-of-consciousness exercise with a flow that had an intensely spiritual momentum. She registered a new zone. According to Karen Fournier, an associate professor of music at the University of Michigan and author of *The Words and Music of Alanis Morissette*, Alanis and songwriting partner Glen Ballard were working on a different piece of music when suddenly their collaboration turned toward this, and they just ran with it. In a blink, it was finalized into what we hear on the album. Imagine what kind of poems might have come out of young Alanis if she knew then what elder Alanis later learned from Schwartz, if young Alanis believed that she truly had no bad parts. Using stream of consciousness as a creative tool, she was able to articulate the arguments of her inner saboteur and thereby give a voice to something she sensed as a bad part of herself.

Stream-of-consciousness writing is a tried-and-true feminist tactic practiced with regularity by such esteemed authors as Virginia Woolf, Jane Austen, and Sylvia Plath. The practice of writing itself becomes more automatic, less judgmental of the honest feelings that appear on the page. The revelation of their otherwise suppressed, hidden, inner lives is part of what makes the style appealing to feminist writers looking to undermine the patriarchal pressure to be well-behaved women. The style merges a sense of third-person narration with first-person interior monologues or external dialogues, for a free but indirect speech that affords more capable agency than that of a single perspective. "Perfect" offers the voice of a parent for those who want to hear that, and the inner voice of Alanis for those who want to hear that. When she sings it now, elder Alanis must feel proud and redeemed, like she's more successfully parenting herself and meeting the needs of this particularly ambitious facet of her inner teenager.

Jamie Grumet's 2019 book, *Modern Attachment Parenting: The Comprehensive Guide to Raising a Secure Child*, attempts to ensure that children grow up with their needs completely met. In her foreword for the book, Alanis self-identifies in her signature as a writer, artist, and activist. She writes that she finds Grumet's work exciting because it openly engages the things that come with the archetypal role of mother: pressure, beauty, overwhelm, maternal fire, the heavy burden of perfectionism, tenderness, and activism. The whole basis of attachment parenting is that children leaving the nest will feel more grounded and ready to do so if they have experienced tons of closeness and secure connection to their caretakers in their formative early years.

This explains a lot about why Gen Xers are so fucked up. Our parents were neither attuned to nor responsive to us. We could cook our own dinner at age seven and had a set of house keys at age nine. No wonder Gen Xers are the demographic backbone supporting this style of parenting, although Alanis cites a long lineage of psychologists who have been studying and developing theories of attachment parenting in different cultures around the world for many years. She has properly studied them. When Alanis writes a foreword, it's in support of generalized movement toward an idea more than an endorsement of a particular author. In this foreword, as in her others, Alanis surmises that individuals working to heal themselves are a cornerstone of the recipe for world peace, if not the whole megillah.

The theme of perfection and its two threads of parenting and spirituality were carried through "Perfect" into 2012, where they blossomed into the *Havoc and Bright Lights* album. The "Guardian" single utilizes the same style of indirect free speech, wherein either a parent is speaking to a child or the speaker is dialoguing with parts of her inner self. This contrasts with the unguarded and exposed feeling of "Spiral," which makes plain that the challenges symptomatic of "Perfect" are at best in remission without a cure. The most the singer can do is walk away from perfectionism toward the generosity and healing of "Empathy." Again, these are all songs that may be addressed to the self, but also to parents or siblings or lovers or friends, and also to the gods or whatever higher energy is out there. This is meant as all-purpose medicine. Alanis offers the main idea, then her fans can lob it at whatever target they each feel it can best assist.

Most of these songs focus on giving everything one can

give, until "Receive" hits in the second-to-last-spot on the album, arguing in favor of setting good boundaries for self-care. Learning to receive, to stop overextending for others and instead pausing to fill up one's own cup, is not easy. Gen Xers are a textbook example here. The stereotype goes that after having raised themselves as best they could, they're no longer able to accept any help or support because they simply don't trust anyone to stick around. Or maybe that's just me—taking care of myself, resenting others for not taking care of me, then bitterly banking on being alone until my prophesy becomes self-fulfilling and I am genuinely isolated. Fortunately, just as Alanis found her husband Souleye, I found my wife Dapper Mindy. As Alanis sings on "'Til You," it feels like we dodged a lot of bullets until we found our person. This is the person that invites us to show our whole self, including the so-called bad parts. Or as she sings on "Empathy," the one by whom we truly feel seen.

The first verse of "Empathy" still admits the prospect that we can never entirely be seen. Alanis sings about holding back some of her parts, including some secret songs, which it is easy to assume she means both literally and figuratively. From *Jagged Little Pill* onward, even casual fans have been aware of her penchant for hidden tracks, for the surplus bubbling over of the many more things she always feels can be said. It can be a struggle to hit the brakes once feelings get flowing, to draw boundaries effectively when using stream of consciousness as a mode of writing. One of the things I personally find enigmatic about the *Havoc and Bright Lights* album is the web of eight bonuses attached to it. That's twenty songs altogether, and at one point before the album came out she had thirty-one tracks to pick from—enough to make a shortish double album quite lengthy. Those eight tracks that were not part of the first commercial release were launched from a few different platforms.

Two were on the deluxe edition of the album, which is a standard upselling ploy. One track that featured her husband was only available on iTunes. Another featuring her husband was bundled with two other bonus tracks into a package only available at Target. Amazon also got one exclusive track, and the eighth was released in Japan. Imagine the sort of hilariously, nefariously data-rich music industry calculation models that produced this marketing strategy. On the one hand, it seems typical of the business. On the other hand, we might worry that execs wanted to spread out the bodies, bury the most spiritually direct recordings like "Guru" and "Magical Child" in a couple of different places, shushing them for fear that they were bankrolling a woo-woo mystic and not wanting to draw attention to ideas both lyrical and sonic that they expected to be commercially less popular.

The woo-woo is evident all the way back to Alanis's first forays into book endorsement. She wrote a foreword to a 2009 yoga book, *Transformative Yoga: Five Keys to Unlocking Inner Bliss*, by her twin brother, Wade Imre Morissette, but the first foreword she wrote was in 2001, for Neale Donald Walsch's *Conversations with God for Teens*. The manner of writing here feels close to the version of Alanis we get in promotional copy related to her music, all lowercase lettering with paragraphs so short as to often be composed of a single sentence. The tone in each of her other forewords is also quite intimate, but this is the only one of them that makes no overtures toward the scholarly. She simply writes about how, alongside the millions of other people who helped land Walsch's first book in the *Conversations with God* series on the bestseller list for one hundred and thirty-five weeks, she was on a quest for spiritual fulfillment, and somebody handed her the book precisely when she was most open to relying upon it.

Alanis and Walsch both grew up Catholic and ended up with an East-West à la carte menu of Zenlike transcendentalism that falls under the heading of New Age spirituality. In some sense, both consider themselves to be modern-day spiritual messengers. Walsch has published about thirty books, and yet of all the titles he could've chosen, Alanis was asked to blurb the one for teens. At the time of the book's publication, she was twenty-seven years old with two albums under her belt. In the foreword, she recalls leaving her religion behind at age twelve and describes how she felt herself resisting the way of life being offered to her by school and figures of authority. She heard messages "of choicelessness, of patriarchy, of there being one singular goal in life toward which our whole lives were to be focused if we wanted to be successful." These are the nightmarishly normative traps evoked by the lyrics to "Perfect." As they say in horror films, the call was coming from inside the house.

4

CHICKEN SHIT

The first two singles launched off *JLP* were both censored: "You Oughta Know" for *fuck* and then "Hand in My Pocket" for *chicken shit*. Radio and MTV slapped a moment of silence over each of these words, the audio equivalent of a shiny piece of duct tape that surely drew more attention to the swearing than it would have gotten otherwise. Judging by "All I Really Want," which happens to contain a longer silence that Alanis deliberately put there for performative effect, her fans are pretty skilled at reading different kinds of silence as forms of attack. Thoughts and feelings flood into spaces that have been cleared out by a silence, a coalescing of forces that collectively provoke a sense of anxiety or insecurity.

Alanis was briefly interviewed by Steve Anderson for his 2005 documentary about the F-bomb, *F**k*. She stated that "it's not used by everybody, so it's a special word. Everybody uses the word 'breakfast,' but not everyone feels so comfortable using the word 'fuck,' so there's an extra power behind it." The taboo against saying it makes it a rarity and there is an additional punch when you use a rare word. She had done another experiment with this in 2000, performing in a two-week off-Broadway run at the Westside Theater in Eve Ensler's *The Vagina Monologues* stage play. Alanis delivered about a third of the monologues, most notably "Reclaiming Cunt," which naturally includes eight C-bombs. Perhaps there is greater permissiveness or social acceptability in deploying the V-word or C-word nowadays, but we still can't say these words on television or radio broadcasts without getting a hefty fine from the Federal Communications Commission.

Unlike "You Oughta Know," "Hand in My Pocket" would be difficult to characterize as an attack. Musically, "Hand in My Pocket" relies on mellow and melodic guitar sustains and the waves of wind coming through her harmonica, whereas "You Oughta Know" is breathless, driven by clipped drumming, and sharp, both vocally and instrumentally. Nobody is humming "You Oughta Know" while they're out walking around with one hand in their pocket, which means the silence the censors threw on top of "Hand in My Pocket" feels different. Their attempt to gloss over "chicken shit" distorts what is otherwise a smooth sonic and lyrical experience.

In a listing song composed almost entirely of binary ontological pairs like sad/laughing, tired/working, and free/focused, the listener ends up mentally rocking back and forth between these separate but related, yet not dualistic, ways of being. These are all pairs, yet she is offering something more multifaceted than a mere thesis and antithesis. The bleeping of "chicken shit" very noticeably leaves "brave" without a pairing, fundamentally preventing the resolution of the line in what has otherwise been a string of beautifully counterbalanced ways that a person might be in tension within themselves. The erasure of "brave's" counterpart, and this censorious impulse in general, is opposed to Morissette's own approach to cognitive dissonance. Her juxtaposing of not-quite-opposites within each line vaults beyond the Hegelian to land in territory that is closer to that of hard-but-friendly Zen koans, where one can feel drunk but be sober at the same time. It's a keen study in nineties ambivalence.

And as "Hand in My Pocket" has proliferated widely across media in the intervening years, each new cover band or television show or film that wants to use it not only has to align with Alanis's values enough to win her approval but also has to decide how best to address the censorship question that will always already be attached to "chicken shit." Of course, parodies that constitute fair use would be exempt from seeking her approval but not necessarily from the censorship question. The river of homages to "Hand in My Pocket" runs very deep, and it's worth our time to wade into several of the parodies, covers, and soundtrack usages to see how they engage with the tactics of the original.

We may be using "chicken shit" as one barometer, yet "Evil Scotsman," the parody by comedian Garry Desmond that is often misattributed to Billy Connolly, blows this out of the water by amusingly deploying "fuck" several times. The song itself is toxic masculine trash, just some guy going on and on about his ten inches and what a badass he is. The backing track is pretty much "Hand in My Pocket," but there are no parallels to speak of in the rhetorical moves of the song or the way it's sung. It's so distant from the original that we can't even ask how it deals with the "chicken shit" lyric. We can only assume that Desmond's self-published album did not have a broad audience beyond the Spanish island of Gran Canaria, where he did a stint as a resident comedian.

The parody song "Snippets" is likewise no more than a

distant cousin to the original. It's a freebie that was released online by British comedians Adam Kay and Suman Biswas under the band moniker Amateur Transplants. Among the excerpts that it samples, this ridiculous mash-up includes bits from Coldplay, U2, Phil Collins, a-ha, and, somehow, even a piece of "Macarena" by Los del Río. It does have a shockingly well-mapped-out agenda, though. Most of the duo's parody songs have medical themes because both of them studied medicine. "Snippets" is meant to mock a medical school that was a rival of the one they attended, and it includes two F-bombs.

By far the best parody is "Hand in a Lightsocket" by Bob Rivers, who has a series of "twisted tunes" that are very much of a piece with the work of "Weird Al" Yankovic. Rivers is a retired rock and roll on-air radio personality who ruled over Seattle's oldies station for twenty-five years. He has both knowledge and chops, and in this parody he takes direct aim at Alanis with a song about her origin—that putting her hand in a light socket begat the style of singing he characterizes as squealing like a swine. No points for feminism there, but he is tactically adept, including the excellent juxtapositions of hip-but-sappy and fried-but-cooking. His critique, given in the first person as if Alanis were the speaker, denigrates her for being horny like a toad and prone to cursing like a sailor. Maybe this implies she's guilty of acting like a man, or like a rock star. Alanis herself has written first-person satirical songs about rock stardom as a wider criticism of celebrity commodity culture, so perhaps we can classify "Hand in a Lightsocket" as a good try on a few levels.

Yet the parodies of "Hand in My Pocket" never quite hit. The tracks feel musically light, though their juxtapositions may be rather serious. One thing these parodies have in common is that they all engage in smack talk—against other bros, against rival schools, against Alanis herself—seeming to go for the aggressive attitude of other songs on *JLP* rather than the voice of "Hand in My Pocket." The other thing they have in common is that they all use a very straightforward version of the backing track that sounds like the original. So, let's turn our attention to what can be done with the musical arrangement. Maybe changing the song composition has different effects vis-à-vis the original while changing the lyrics seems to fall flat, comparatively.

There have been a few minor covers of "Hand in My Pocket" by a handful of bands, plus two major covers that aired on widely watched television shows. Canadian country-pop singer MacKenzie Porter was only five when the song debuted. In 2020, she added a second guitar and downshifted from the fun fuzz of the original into something less gritty, more Nashvillian, while not tipping over into a full-blown twang. When Canadian punk-pop band Seaway covered the song in 2016, the slightly more up-tempo cadence added a buoyancy to the overall vibe that was consistent with a genuine homage. All the members of this band were still in diapers when "Hand in My Pocket" came out, and both singers in the video can plainly be seen checking the lyrics on their cell phones as they go.

A perhaps equally genuine but far less adequate vibe is that of the Miami-based hard rock band Atom Smash, whose 2013 cover starts out with a few cool sustains that tease the prospect of Eastern influence, then quickly spirals downward into a distantly psychedelic vocal droning combined with thrash metal moments that ultimately do not seem to relate to the context of the original whatsoever.

There is a certain amount of unthinking Crosby, Stills, and Nash-ification in a cover like this. It's a soulless yet technically solid execution in which the song is clearly a representative sample of the band's musical stylings but utterly detached from the original: in dialogue with the source material only by virtue of lyrics or chords, without the meat of meanings or feelings on those bones. Bless their ham-fisted hearts.

All three of those covers were able to keep in the "chicken shit" line, in part because they avoided radio play. They went under the radar. Despite the widely differing genres of these musicians, something Alanis was doing appealed to them. "Hand in My Pocket" doesn't continue to proliferate only among singers, but also among actors who can sing. Around the twentieth anniversary of *JLP* in 2015 and 2016, two of the most popular television series at that time—*Glee* and *Transparent*—both rolled out very emotive covers of the song. It's at this point that we must briefly pause to acknowledge the fact that I identify as a queer and Alanis does not, though her music helped me to cope with clarifying my identity when my instincts told me it would be safer to simply censor it. Bleeping out a cuss word runs parallel to closeting queerness. Both are about keeping the popular conversation palatable, about policing deviations from the norm. So Alanis helped me to be a lot less chicken shit back in the day, and wedging "Hand in My Pocket" into contemporary popular conversation leverages the norm-breaking model of her allyship in at least these two televised instances. The introverted yet winking bravery on display when she is confronted with censorship can be gleaned from the song's deployment in these fictional contexts. These modern storylines and characters successfully lean on her song to fill out their emotional content, which is getting more explicitly queer all the time rather than merely implicitly queer coded. What I'm saying is, there is no question now that Alanis is a queer icon.

The show *Glee* is an hour-long musical television series featuring teenagers who form a glee club at school. The show is widely respected for its guest performers and unique show-choir transformations of current radio hits. It's widely beloved by nerds of all ages for depicting the struggles of being different and feeling like an outsider, whether that meant Artie's wheelchair or the fledging lesbian love story between two cheerleaders. There is a special moment in episode three of season six when Santana sings to Brittany before proposing they get married. This "Jagged Little Tapestry" episode mashes up "Hand in My Pocket" with Carole King's "I Feel the Earth Move." The entire glee club cheers for them and their love. We leapfrog over the problem of the chicken shit line by dropping some Carole King in that slot instead, maintaining the necessity of a TV-14 rating.

Transparent is a half-hour drama about a dysfunctional family in Los Angeles. It's rated TV-MA and considered pioneering in its exploratory and supportive focus on many aspects of queer culture, especially stemming from the main character's identity as a trans woman. Her ex-wife and best friend, played by Judith Light, closes the season three finale with a one-woman show on a cruise ship. Accompanied only by a piano in cabaret style, Shelly sings "Hand in My Pocket" tentatively and a little ridiculously at first but grows louder and taller with each verse until it really does seem to be as the lyrics say: she will be fine. There's a faint whiff of Sinatra's "My Way" about her performance, and as she sings the chicken shit bit inside the darkened dinner theater, her son is serving memento mori, dumping an urn full of ashes off the side of the boat into the churning waves.

The song serves as a toast, a celebration of the uncertain road ahead. Santana, Brittany, and Shelly are dusting themselves off and getting on with whatever joys they can find. These are queer stories, but they are also all having a graduation of sorts. "Hand In My Pocket" reflects the pendulum swings of these coming-of-age tales.

There are four other particularly clear-cut examples here that we can more briefly examine, the first two from television and the second two in films. In 1998, "Hand in My Pocket" was intended to be the theme song for *Dawson's Creek* and was used in the unaired pilot. Alanis gave only short-term permission for its use, so the studio turned to Paula Cole out of necessity once the show was greenlit. The show is about a girl next door caught between two prospective partners who are not quite opposites. In 2021, the song appeared in the *Mare of Easttown* pilot, in which Kate Winslet plays a small-town Pennsylvania detective solving the murder of a young girl while beset by a relentless string of the usual working-class personal and public servant problems. She limps into the local bar and Alanis plays in the background as Mare considers whether to screw a hot professor who is guest lecturing at the nearby college. The song makes the case.

In 2017, Greta Gerwig used the song in her solo directorial debut *Lady Bird*, a widely acclaimed coming-of-age film about a girl from Sacramento who is beleaguered by her domineering mother and hoping to escape to New

York City after graduation. "Hand in My Pocket" plays on the radio as Lady Bird's father drives her to school, a rare moment of quietude and support in her otherwise stereotypically hectic and dramatic teenage Catholic schoolgirl existence. She marvels to her father that the song was written in just ten minutes, evidence that a few moments can change everything or that her own talents might prove to be equally unstoppable. He smiles and says he believes it, an affirmation of both the spoken and the unspoken.

For the final example, suffice it to say that in 2020, a gigantic oversight in the universe of nineties popular culture was properly corrected when the mostly awful movie *The Craft: Legacy* included Alanis on the soundtrack, thereby resolving the problem of the original 1996 cult classic film *The Craft* somehow not containing any of her music. I suspect the overlap between superfans of Alanis and superfans of *The Craft* is somewhere north of ninety percent. "Hand in My Pocket" serves as the shorthand reference for a common emotional state among sane but overwhelmed strong female leads, showing up to provide some anti-heroic ambiance for complex women who do not have the time or space to be chicken shit.

5

ALL THE INFORMATION

Sometimes I spend a few minutes thinking about how best to calculate the number of men I had to get beyond to be here, existing on this page in the present moment. Not just the ones I fucked so they'd help me or the ones I fucked so they'd leave me alone. Not just the ones who worked half as hard as me or the ones who were twice as dumb as me, but also those who advised me to smile more, and their wives, and their jokes. Their sense of entitlement to my meal ticket, their unearned privilege of using me as a puppet, their arbitrary power over my ass regenerating like the agents in *The Matrix*. Any girl who listens to "Right Through You" understands that it contains a series of checkboxes for all the awful grownup types that Alanis had already met.

Alanis grew up to be the very successful Miss Thing, but she is still a thing—the monstrosity inherently associated with being a woman. According to Jess Zimmerman's *Women and Other Monsters: Building a New Mythology*, women are going to be treated as monstrous no matter what we do and the inevitability of this means we must work with our monstrosity rather than fight it or pretend it isn't there. This is especially true for creatives—those of us with generative instincts to build a manifesto out of the facets of our lives that sadden and terrify men who don't know how to witness us, don't know how to read us or love us or employ us. They can't handle all the information before they turn us away. Let those men keep fearing when women like Alanis put their shoulder to the wheel.

As we saw in the early chapters focused on parallels with literary characters, every woman who truly serves excellence leaves a trail of carnage in her wake. Not that we want to hurt people, although hurt people do often hurt people. It's just that for a woman to succeed in her own life, she first must get beyond the very many standard males who simply prefer that she not do so. My resolve to do no harm is often at odds with my resolve to take no shit. Even though I could go on and on in a litany of the bleached bones and hollowed-out shells of the many copies of Mr. Man lying there on the road behind me that make it hard to glance in the rearview mirror sometimes, let us recall that the particular forms of masculinity indicted by "Right Through You" are primarily enabled by their infusion into a capitalist system, which we might usefully narrow to focus on the music business.

In this case, Alanis understands that the record company execs are appraising her prospective commodification, and she argues that this is at the expense of her humanity. In other words, she feels invisible. The song performs an "I'm rubber, you're glue" conceit of reversal and leaves the exec feeling invisible instead: "Now that I'm a zillionaire / You scan the credits for your name / And wonder why it's not there." She goes right through him, gets beyond him. The music business has always defaulted to a baseline of dismissiveness regarding the talent of female musicians, treating them like a joke or a child, even as they are being used to generate massive profits. The harsh evaluation of this tension performed by the lyrics is a clever counter to the appraisals that were placed on Alanis, wherein the pot and the kettle succeeded in calling each other black. Yet this was a gamble when she wrote it because she was not Miss Thing at the time, so the song's revenge moment was intended more as campy self-deprecation, due to no one expecting the album to rocket her to such a level.

JLP ended up undercutting the classic commodification model, as the marketing department, hilariously, had to scramble to get out in front of the album's instantly enormous fan base. For example, Alanis ended up on the covers of both *Spin* and *Rolling Stone* that November, an extremely rare feat usually reserved for recently deceased icons. The album was still several weeks away from being shipped out to record stores or even other radio stations when KROQ Los Angeles played the first single on air for the first time and the phones immediately started ringing. The woman we must credit for this is Lisa Worden, who was at that moment in the very first year of her two decades as music director for the legendary alternative rock radio station. It was apparent that the album had a momentum all its own as the execs at Warner belatedly fought to steer it.

But all of this treats Alanis like an artist in a vacuum, analyzing her on her singular merits as if they had no wider context. The nineties are known as "the decade of women in rock," and it's of course difficult to excavate *JLP* from the amber of that sticky gimmick. For starters, there was the ancient dictum that only one female musician shall appear on a rock radio station's playlist at any given time. The scarcity vibes were immense, each team vying to push their productized human through the few doors that were open. Women who wanted to cooperate with each other for the sake of their art forms instead of competing for the sake of their sales figures had a hell of a time convincing their execs to let it happen. The message I got as a high school student and fledgling creative watching Sarah McLachlan put together Lilith Fair is that women who rock are at best considered separate but equal—which is of course never properly equitable. Given how deeply I felt my femaleness and my feminism at that time, being a writer seemed easier than being a rock star.

Look how far into this book we got without putting Alanis into a sentence with Liz Phair—one the queen of mainstream magazines and one the queen of indie college radio, both stomping the demand for Sheryl Crow and throwing scraps to Paula Cole while Melissa Etheridge was taking a break to make babies and Ani DiFranco was establishing Righteous Babe Records, et cetera. And that's just a handful of only the white women. No artist is an island: they suss out networks and form cohorts and mentor each other just like in any other profession. As much as I'm overcome with a swoony urge to rhapsodize on the siren wailings of Alanis and Sinéad O'Connor as two peas in a pod, a lot of this work to contextualize women artists feels like it does as much harm as good. The passage of time has not lessened this hunch. Every time *JLP* has an anniversary, there are a handful of think pieces on why it was the greatest album of its time and then a deluge of unkind retorts for which titles like "Ten 90s Albums More Feminist than Alanis Morissette's *Jagged Little Pill*" from *Collapse Board* are typical.

This notion that one could be "more feminist" presumes that women can be located along a spectrum of palatability, the monstrous reality of riot grrrls at one end and the pleasing fiction of "Stepford wives" at the other. The Stepford wives are utterly compliant robots based on the female characters from Ira Levin's 1975 satirical horror story of the same name, and this excerpt from Elizabeth Wurtzel's 1999 classic *Bitch: In Praise of Difficult Women* gives a sweetly idyllic description of riot grrrls: "So sometime in the early nineties, the girls all by themselves, with no assistance from any international conglomerates, invented the Riot Girl movement, starting punk-rock bands and fanzines in suburban garages and rec rooms just like boys used to do, linking up with other girls in disparate cities like Washington, D.C., and Vancouver and Olympia and Toronto through Internet chat rooms and newsletters. And they forged a manifesto."

This continuum of acceptability is applied to every facet of the musician's work, from the way they interact with execs and promoters to the way their products and performances are judged by media and fans. Alanis somehow reached this minimum threshold of acceptability, leading English professor Sara Marcus to theorize about the transmutation of ideology from the original riot grrrls of Bikini Kill: "Some women are never going to access Bikini Kill, but they're aware of Hole. Some women aren't aware of Hole, but they're listening to Alanis Morissette. Now we're at a third-generation degraded copy, and at the same time, there's an embrace of anger and obscenity that does something for people. Even the Spice Girls are like a fourth-generation degraded copy from Riot Grrrl." We can admit that the feminist messaging gets watered down, but we must admire that the seedling still survives with enough to grow on. I worked backward from Alanis to Hole to Bikini Kill until I found myself on an intellectual patio overlooking the outside of the system. Men dominate every slice of the system, not just its musical output. Early on, the only female rock critic I knew of was Jessica Hopper. Then I worked backward to Ellen Willis and over to Lisa Robinson.

Robinson, who has spent more than forty years covering the music business, offers an overview of the myriad suffocating effects this continuum of acceptability has had in her memoir *Nobody Ever Asked Me about the Girls: Women, Music, and Fame*. The chapters are organized by theme as Robinson spills the tea on female troubles trending in the industry, from hair and makeup to drugs and marriage. Alanis makes brief appearances in the chapters on ambition, fame, sex, business, influence, and age. In the ambition chapter, Katy Perry says her friends would sneak her secular pop music like Alanis's. Perry would then go on to work with Glen Ballard, who was the writing partner for Alanis on her first two albums. Her nastiest critics said that Ballard was the true creative brain responsible for *JLP*.

You can look for the writer or producer credits for many albums made since 1982 and find Ballard's name. Musicians commonly work with one songwriting partner for one or two albums and then, whether those succeed or fail, at some point the stakeholders from A&R will want to "shake things up," "go in a different direction," "not limit their growth," or (insert your favorite break-up cliché here). Ballard did not leave due to any drama; he was simply committed elsewhere, working on Lisa Marie Presley's debut. Nor was he replaced with another songwriting partner or another producer. So with *Under Rug Swept* in 2002, for the first time in her life Alanis alone was credited as writer and producer.

A musical partnership of the caliber of Alanis and Ballard's is undoubtedly a kind of marriage. In her lyrics about romance, it's within the ballpark to consider that some of them may also reflect, in a parallel way, on the songwriting partnership with Ballard. For example, one hopes he isn't the abusive mentor addressed in "Hands Clean," sweeping his ancient misdeeds under the rug. Perhaps he was a part of "Precious Illusions," a song about a soft-landing place that nevertheless prevents the singer from achieving fuller self-confidence and independence. Alanis is used to Ballard being in the flow space of her creations; used to him being the first listener for her lyrics and melodies; in the habit of iterating her ideas based on how they bounce back mediated by his reactions. No more man in the room, just all the selves that compose Alanis.

Against the preceding notion of mapping women onto a sliding scale of palatability, I want to offer the binary pass-fail prospect of cartoonist Alison Bechdel's iconic test. In 1985, Bechdel posited that when it comes to representing women in film, she is looking for a movie with two women in it, and in the film they must discuss anything other than a man. Maybe all the selves Alanis brought to the making of *Under Rug Swept* can be put into dialogue with each other and maybe that conversation can be about something that isn't focused on the men in her orbit. Let us get beyond them.

And yet this whole line of inquiry fails the test because it revolves around the palpability of Ballard's absence from the album. Amusingly, *Under Rug Swept* was criticized for being about more of the same *JLP* themes, i.e., kvetching about relationships. If the two albums are so much alike, it seems silly to give that much credit to Ballard for the first one. On the other hand, it's not wildly speculative to assume that there must've been moments during her work on *Under Rug Swept* when Alanis asked herself what Ballard would have done.

We can still get beyond him via less literal interpretation of the music. Although her first foray into solo writing and producing appears on the surface to yield content in the same vein as her earlier work, the experiences of those intervening seven years gave Alanis a different outlook on her familiar themes, according to Karen Fournier's analysis. After a series of travels to India, Eastern Europe, the Middle East, and the Navajo Nation on humanitarian missions of cultural exchange, Alanis came to believe that her personal problems were parallel to geopolitical problems, rooted as they were in the same less-than-empathic approaches to relationship building and conflict resolution.

She told Jennifer Vineyard at *MTV News* in 2002 that she sees these travels and her own problems as being of a piece with a single theme: "There's a thread of continuity, subject matter-wise, that permeates not only every trip I take, but every interaction I have," and "the sense of community the Navajo people really focus on" is similar to the sense of community she felt on tour in the Middle East. Alanis pours this notion into the lyrics for "Utopia," imagining that "We'd open our arms / We'd all jump in / We'd all coast down into safety nets." She continued to write songs that appeared to be about one shitty dude at a time, but she had come to view the songs as microcosms of planetary miscommunication and she was not interested in writing more obviously political songs instead.

All conflicts were one conflict, a fact that she expected

her fans could infer without waiting for more explicit information, extrapolating a wider sense of morality from a sample of a few bad romances. The album tour was named Toward Our Union Mended, from the chorus line in "A Man." This song is unique in her catalog for its empathy exercise: in it, Alanis adopts the voice of an everyman, specifically the type targeted by her music who considers himself to have been "crucified by enraged women," yet he is nevertheless depicted as working toward their more perfect union. Alanis decided to believe that adversaries in command of threatening forces were also negotiating in good faith. This is an evolutionary leap from her view of Mr. Man back in the day.

6

BELIEVE IN SOMETHING

My mother was Jewish but not raised in a temple, and my father quit going to church as soon as his father would let him, so they made no effort whatsoever to establish religious practices for the four kids in our household, though they did make time to heartily disapprove of all my à la carte experimentation with Eastern philosophies and to confiscate any objects in my bedroom that looked the least bit witchy. By contrast, Alanis was raised by devoutly Catholic parents who went to mass every Sunday. She went to school at Holy Family Catholic for elementary and Immaculata High for middle, then got her diploma from Glebe Collegiate Institute, whose Latin motto is *in alta tende*—aim at things on high. The school's mascot is a gryphon, a fantastically contradictory animal that is part lion and part eagle.

On the one hand, Alanis wanted to engage in all the sexy deviance and moderate shenanigans that are the natural right of all teenagers in North America. On the other hand, there were consequences for girls in the nineties. The merits and disadvantages of her Catholic upbringing are described in the song "Forgiven," emphasizing her experience in getting punished differently for her sins simply because she was a girl. As a result, she understood how gender roles are institutionalized by religion as it was used in her schooling and in her church activities. The lyrics ask some important questions about redemption, yet acknowledge that these questions feel a bit stupid. Karen Fournier points out that, as in the early music videos of Madonna before her, Alanis would sometimes be sporting oversized crucifixes as either earrings or a necklace while acting in a flirty, modern way, jumping into fountains and such, that ran contrary to the religious iconography she was wearing. Her conceptualization of spirituality allows for skepticism to play a role in the structuring of belief. She sings that "what I learned I rejected but I believe again," not in the traditional sense of using doubt to pressure-test and ultimately harden arguments in favor of the church, but in the more expansive sense of being able to hold two ideas in conflict with each other in her head at the same time.

Alanis has said the Catholic Church is toxic, yet she has also said that she credits her singing career to it. Her love of candles and aromatherapy is well known, even if her use of these has come to feel secular from our contemporary viewpoint. She practices meditation every day in a special room of her house designed for that purpose, and thinks of the space as where she goes to tune in to her emotions. These are rituals and ceremonies that consistently convey a spiritual inclination despite her accompanying uncertainties. The ballad "Forgiven" expresses a more complex assemblage of emotions than mere anger at the church. Alanis wrote this before she made her pilgrimage to India, yet we can speculate that much of the bliss she found there was drawn in by the spiritual sensibility she brought with her. It is easy to understand that *JLP* is constantly pointing out multifarious hypocrisies, but "Forgiven" demonstrates that she would like to be gracious in the face of the hypocrisies without necessarily granting exoneration or acquittal to the priests. Without mercy, she would be no better than those she has criticized. The question is what it takes to achieve this grace, and the answer is not to just play it cool.

When people talk about the coolness of nineties apathy, they are not talking about Alanis—she felt her contradictory feelings and told us all about them. Romanticizing this coolness glosses over how much anxiety is needed to successfully perform apathy, worrying so much about whether one is worrying too much. The tautological nature of apathy makes clear that it isn't one feeling, but a feedback loop between the lived experience of anxiety and the social perception of coolness. By contrast, *JLP* is a master class in what English professor and influential cultural critic Lauren Berlant would later pioneer as affect theory, busting the culture for its psychological undercurrents rather than accepting at face value that what everybody said about how they didn't care was the truth of how they felt.

For me, living through the nineties was confusing because I constantly felt both strongly positive and strongly negative, and when feeling strongly negative sometimes felt utterly helpless to do anything about it as an unresourced queer teenager in the suburbs. The ambivalence I felt was generated primarily by systems other than religious ones, but we're still talking about the destructive power of norms that congeal in the practices found within any system, whether religious or secular. The unthinkingness of these norms and the equally vacuous policing of them is what allowed dudes like Beavis and Butthead and Bill and Ted to skate through their fictional lives. They always lucked into a last-minute escape, but those near-miss catastrophes are a solid indicator that we can't just sum up the nineties as a time of indifference and let it go at that.

"Forgiven" fundamentally grapples with the question of what to do about postmodern illogics, where the priest says one thing and Alanis watches her brothers do the opposite without consequences, yet if she steps a toe in their direction she is policed back into the straight and narrow line. In pointing out struggles with her religious upbringing, Alanis refuses apathy. Apathy seems to come from nowhere, so it's not cool for her to admit to struggling. It would almost be a violation of apathy to justify where one's apathy comes from. Sure, reality bites, but one cannot exist simply by standing firm in the awkward position that this lifetime is all meaningless. To characterize the nineties as ambivalent means that not only did we feel strongly, we also felt pulled in opposite directions. Berlant would say that even our feelings are a matter of relations, so apathy—blankness, or performing the affect of not having any affect—stems from this relation to our daily living among other humans in which we push one aspect of our emotions aside for the convenience of faking a resolution of contradictory feelings.

The nineties feeling of ambivalence derived from various institutions that remain invested in normativity, like Maverick Records or the Catholic Church, cannot be usefully pointed at because the performative contradictions they engage in are already too much with us. We know the music business exploits female singers, yet we fork over the cash for their albums knowing the execs will take a massive cut because that's the only avenue by which we get to witness their art. We've been participating in the fomentation of certain normative tensions for hundreds of years by surrendering to the desirability of stability and success they present to us rather than accepting a more precarious existence made up of threats and consequences. Belief, even or perhaps especially once it has stiffened into normativity, is our oxygen. We all have our reasons to breathe it. Or it's like the idea that we cannot understand the ocean because we're swimming in it. That's a mystical and sort of Buddhist maneuver against the institutionalization of belief, and it requires us to do as Alanis does, forgiving others and ourselves for being hypocrites.

In "Forgiven," Alanis offers a critique of her experience with the church. The church system that uses beliefs to police gender roles in society might view this song as an attack, but a critique isn't necessarily an attack. It's more akin to the Buddhist strategy of noting. Alanis was merely pointing out that this is the water we're all floating around in or the air that we're all breathing. Music critics may have portrayed Alanis as being worried or pissed off about the church, but perhaps she wasn't worried as much as simply existentially embedded. Regardless of her beliefs or the priests' beliefs, both are using their beliefs to create feelings within themselves. The feelings are what we need to follow, because feeling is a genuine thing that happens inside each of us that ought to be better conveyed and communicated.

Alanis theorizes her feelings. "Forgiven" attempts to wield her critique of the church as productively as the church has wielded its Christianity, with the singer intoning "in the name of the Father, the Skeptic and the Son." In the moment of feeling at an impasse between her desire to meet the norms and to cast them out of the temple of her life, her admission of anxiety in the scenario breaks the surface tension. Her critique admits that a lot of what goes on in church is meaningless justification for some violent and destructive malarky, as her "brothers they never went blind for what they did / But I may as well have." Her feeling of unfairness is predicated on how this traditional system treats women. "Forgiven" is a pressure-release valve for a thing Alanis can't get out of: "You know how us Catholic girls can be." She wants to be forgiven for this critique and she wants to forgive the Catholic Church, acknowledging and therefore momentarily making palatable the hypocrisy of each of us and the systems in which we participate.

It's not that Alanis represents any kind of more authentic self. We might say that she, being neither fully performative nor fully authentic, occasionally achieves a spiritual distance. Like all of us, she simply has feelings about the day-to-day work that she does and the norms she encounters while searching along her own path for contentment. Each of us is going to invent whatever pleases us to the extent that the system allows us to do that. We could justify any value system if we just limit the scope of it enough to understand what one person's individual ideology might be. What's good for you, your household, neighborhood, state, nation, or planet might not be good for somebody else's. The beauty of Alanis's critique is that it helps us blow off the steam of anxiety while we're engaged in performative contradiction on a constant basis. "Forgiven" points a finger at the absurdity of our existential predicament. When we're caught in a trap, as we all are in this life bookended by birth and death, there's an immense value to just letting the kettle blow its top for a minute.

The alternative is to be a nihilist, somehow obliterating this world and then building your own universe that can in whatever way more truly aim at things on high. This is not exactly possible, though fiction writers in Hollywood like to take a stab at it. Enter writer and director Kevin Smith, who cast Alanis in the role of God in *Dogma* in 1999 and then again, very briefly, at the end of *Jay and Silent Bob Strike Back* in 2001. The basic premise of the fantasy comedy that is *Dogma* is that if two angels enter a church in New Jersey, it will bring on the apocalypse. Alanis, as God, has banished Matt Damon's Loki and Ben Affleck's Bartleby to Wisconsin because they were insubordinate.

The fallen angels are trying to exploit a loophole in Catholic dogma by finding a meandering way of proving the fallibility of God so they can get back into Heaven—even though the glory of Heaven is predicated in part on God's infallibility, thus requiring the fallen angels to believe two opposing ideas at the same time. Ever the good guy, Loki realizes this and doesn't want to selfishly pursue the end of all creation. But Bartleby, ever the jackass, gets really close to stepping through the church's doors after about two hours of very convoluted and highly amusing antics, featuring an ensemble cast that includes the iconic atheist George Carlin as the cardinal of the church in Jersey. But just as Bartleby opens the doors, God emerges out of the strobe lights and fog. Bartleby falls to his knees, crying and apologetic. They hug it out and then God kills him with the sound of her voice.

Yeah, he just stands there while God opens her mouth and issues a gigantic sonic boom that explodes first Bartleby's head and then his body, which fall to the ground while his soul is presumably restored to Heaven as he originally wanted. When Jason Mewes as recurring character Jay goes off on one of his "what's all this about" rants in classic Jay fashion, God shushes him and kisses his cheek. She smiles big and then cleans up all the carnage in the street without moving or talking. Just your basic miracle work. Then she lays hands on a dead character, not only resurrecting her from death but also gifting her with an immaculate pregnancy, before enjoying herself by doing a headstand against a nearby tree. Alanis steals the scene without uttering a single word. The Catholic League for Religious and Civil Rights, which does not have a strong record of understanding satirical works of art, condemned the film as blasphemy. At the time, Smith was a practicing Catholic who went to church every Sunday.

The View Askewniverse, so far comprising about a dozen Kevin Smith films with overlapping characters and plot references, is truly not any better or worse than what we think of as the real world. It's not more or less delusional than anything else we have believed. Because I was not raised with any religion, I was never quick to cling to and thus be blinded by the Catholic specifics as laid out in "Forgiven." Instead, I was invigorated by the surreal possibilities of simultaneously rejecting and believing in something. So, I did.

7

WHEN THE SMOKE CLEARS

JLP turned twenty in 2015, and Alanis spent six months of the following year writing a total of twenty-one weekly advice columns for the "Life and Style" section of the *Guardian*. The range of subjects she covered was broad and included challenges in romance, parenting, careers, and so on. Editors chose to introduce her in their very British way as the new "agony aunt." To get at the origin of this phrase and its contemporary meaning, we must do as we did in chapter 2 and consult the ancient Greeks. "Agon" refers not only to a painful mental or physical struggle of the soul but also to competition. In archaic mythology, Agon is a deity related to the spirits of rivalry and victory, Zelos and Nike. In modern times, agonism is a branch of socio-political theory that offers a framework for debates about democracy. Feminist agonists, like legal theorist and political science professor Bonnie Honig, believe that because reality is a perpetual contest, we must strive to focus on its affirmative results. When the smoke clears, any outcome of a particular contest should generate growth, truth, and transcendence for the agonized. Win or lose, you learn.

The letter in the first advice column is from a woman worried she is about to tip over into having an emotional affair. Alanis offers several paragraphs more in the spirit of "here's what I've done in such a situation" than in pronouncements of “you should.” She tells the second letter writer “setting a boundary is not being confrontational.” The third letter is from a fourteen-year-old girl and Alanis confirms that she shares the same needs as the girl. Each of the twenty-one letters receives a supportively constructive and fairly casual reply of a few paragraphs, making a gesture at empathy and then recommending a course of action driven by Alanis’s informal but extensive study as an armchair psychologist.

These replies show that Alanis consistently values direct communication of needs and argues for avoiding resentments that poison the well. She approves of asking for help and frequently points out how things that feel burdensome are instead gifts from the universe. Her column recommends a lot of books about parenting and the importance of expressing “nonjudgmental interest” in the weird stuff other people think or do. Alanis never says there’s only one way out of any problem and she never labels a problem as unusual. She admits that she and her husband have gone to couples therapy, that she had postnatal depression, and that she is in recovery from her three primary addictions, to love, food, and work. The darkest moment is in the April 1, 2016, column when she characterizes herself as “someone who turned to people and substances to keep a lifestyle in place that was not good for my nervous system, out of mere survival.”

The notion of assurance turns up repeatedly—Alanis assuring the letter writer that things will turn out just fine, the writer assuring other people involved in their drama that they mean no harm, and of course the self-assurance needed to move forward in life. Even Alanis extricating herself from the final (June 2016) column for the *Guardian* hinges on assurance: "This is my last column—I'm taking a break to have a baby and focus on being a mother. Thank you so much for sharing your stories and challenges with me. I have been deeply moved by your bravery and willingness to ask tough questions, and I will miss you."

This assurance is in some sense contrary to agonism, where the only assured thing is the struggle. Her sign-off demonstrates a love for the challenges of life. In modern parlance, we might say Alanis leans in when facing struggle. She generally recommends deepening connections or understanding, as opposed to trying to break away. *JLP* documents many kinds of interpersonal conflict, yet the message is never oriented toward breaking free of these struggles. Neglect and avoidance are never her answers. The songs aren't in the vein of the Animals' "We Gotta Get Out of This Place" or the Ramones' "I Wanna Be Sedated," because in true agonistic fashion, Alanis accepts the existential belief that life necessarily includes struggle. This is akin to the Buddhist notion that humans always suffer because of their attachments to objects, events, and other humans.

Yet, somehow, we continue to live and love, even as we are crying, losing, bleeding, and screaming—because we learn. Although "You Learn" was the fourth single released off *JLP*, it falls in the exact middle of the track listing and should be properly considered the true theme and anchoring message of the album. According to the thirteen hundred setlists from her shows collected by setlist.fm since 1987, "You Learn" has been played at about 58 percent of her shows. Rather than get into mapping its movement within the setlists of various tours and the significance of where it lands in the lineup for any particular night, we can jump right to a singular positioning of the song that entirely makes the case: "You Learn" is the closing number of the *Jagged Little Pill* Broadway musical.

Because it is the largest and most updated wellspring of commentary on the original album, we'll need to return repeatedly to different aspects of the Broadway musical for analysis in later chapters. To underscore the significance of "You Learn" here, the key thing to know is that the finale of the musical returns all characters to the stage, bloody but unbowed while steering toward resolution in their various struggles. Even the press kit for the show declares, "You live, you learn, you remember what it's like to feel truly human . . . at *Jagged Little Pill*." The final number is a catharsis of epic proportions because we in the audience have come to view the show's plot twists in light of our own parallel plights. We can leave the theatre with a feeling of assurance, not that we'll be able to simply shake off our burdens but that we are of necessity striving like the characters on stage to make peace with the struggles that continually haunt each one of us.

"You Learn" effectively delivers closure to the musical because both the song and the show are about how to not feel victimized by our own poor choices or the violence of others toward us. "You Learn" also anchors the album by providing a title reference to a jagged little pill in the third line of the first verse. Nobody wants to swallow a jagged little pill. It sticks in the craw. Maybe it also cuts, whether as a microaggression or a major trauma. It rarely feels little, and it definitely doesn't feel good, yet Alanis sings about how it does feel good as it swims around in the stomach. Eventually the dust settles, as the pill of our struggles great and small dissolves in our system and we continue to carry it around as part of what defines us. The jagged little pill is the superheroic origin story of Alanis and of each of us. The key is transforming our struggles by learning from them, squeezing out their lessons to make lemonade from the lemons. These lessons define our character. A lifelong learner has an endless capacity to grow from struggle.

For me, the jagged little pill has always been a supreme sigil of hauntology. A sigil is a type of symbol that is used in magic. It's a pictorial signature of a spirit, sort of a ghost's coat of arms. As for hauntology, it is not simply the study of haunting. The term was first used by French philosopher Jacques Derrida as a portmanteau of two words: haunting plus ontology. The jagged little pill is emotional baggage that I continue to carry around from the disasters and foolishness of my youth in the nineties. Things like parental neglect or homophobic discrimination that were done to me, things like competitiveness of mind or weaponization of body that I did to myself, these leave traces that haunt me by shaping the ways I exist in the world. The ghosts of my past inform my present approach to life—in a healthier manner each day, if I am focused and lucky.

Derrida introduced hauntology in his 1993 book *Specters of Marx*. This is kind of a jokey title, a riff on Karl Marx's proclamation in *The Communist Manifesto* that the specter of communism is haunting Europe, whereby Derrida turns Marx into a ghost haunting the subsequent history of Western thought. Marx was afraid that his values would remain ghosts, never implemented as actual communism, whereas Derrida took a longer and less urgently political view that Marx's thinking has itself come to be an always present absence. Hauntology refers to the recurrence or endurance of tensions from our social and cultural past. The ontological status of the specter is that it never fully arrives and never fully departs. The jagged little pill is spectral, and this book project exists because I am haunted by it. My writing about Alanis is hauntological. So too is the haters' impulse to dismiss her work as merely angry or merely feminist. *JLP* sticks to them and leaves a trace. The album and the artist refuse to go away even when critics refuse to learn from them.

The hauntological is also a music genre, consisting mostly of electronic bands from the United Kingdom and other purveyors of chill ambient vibe sounds or nostalgic sampling of music from old television shows and other familiar pop culture artifacts. In 2022, Alanis released an album that can easily be classified as part of this musical genre. *The Storm before the Calm* contains eleven tracks of instrumental meditation music, the shortest of which is five and a half minutes and some of which reach the twelve-minute mark. In the press release announcing the album, Alanis said that she and her collaborator, Dave Harrington, only met face to face once and otherwise worked exclusively through video chatting. She made the album during the pandemic and describes it in the press release as a "multi-layered life raft" that she hopes will "serve as a catalyst, a soothing, a glimpse of awakening. an honoring. an objectivity. a wordless partner in healing. a place to land. inquire. breathe. notice. one in which you are held." This is an excellent description of the spectral as medicine.

If we choose to accept this medicine, to learn from the struggles that haunt us, a ghost becomes more like a guardian angel. Alanis acknowledges that her song "Guardian" was written to speak not only to her newborn son but also to her own inner child. She wore gigantic white wings in the music video as a hat tip to the classic Wim Wenders film *Wings of Desire*, which was celebrating its own twenty-fifth anniversary at the time. This video makes a link between the role of guardian angel and parent, whereas her much earlier homage to Wenders, "Uninvited," makes a link between guardian angel and romantic partner: Alanis wrote that hit single for the soundtrack to Brad Silberling's 1998 film *City of Angels*, which was a reboot of *Wings of Desire* with a somewhat sadder conclusion.

"Uninvited" conveys the quandaries of the plot quite well. Nic Cage plays Seth, a guardian angel who falls in love with Meg Ryan, as surgeon Maggie Rice, while she is failing to save someone he watches over. Because angels have free will, Seth decides to fall to earth to pursue Maggie. They have a very short amount of blissfully mortal time together before she is killed in a car crash, leaving the freshly arrived Seth to sort out how to make the most of his new life alone. The film and its song are literally about a haunting, and the song structure conveys this through a melody that explores themes of nostalgia, memory, and the specters of the past via a dark and brooding atmosphere. As the intensity builds toward an instrumental climax, the musical arrangement of atmospheric elements, including strings and subtle electronic textures, adds to the song's moody and introspective feel. Its overall melancholia makes the song classifiable as an example of the hauntological genre of music.

This was the first single Alanis made after *JLP*, and it's driven by four lingering piano notes that build to a spooky climax as the tension rises in the lyrics over a decision that must be made. Seth as angelic specter was uninvited to the mortal life Maggie led, and much of the turmoil of the film centers on her efforts to understand and believe in the possibilities represented by his existence. She must make a leap of faith to approach her own hauntedness in a more vulnerable and open manner, and ultimately she invites him into her life. After she extends this invitation, both learn a lot about happiness in the short time that they are alive together and afterward when they have switched roles because she's an angel and he's a mortal. Yet "Uninvited" doesn't end on a note of whatever kind of joy they learned to achieve. In the song, Alanis ends without an ending, by asking for a moment to deliberate. Just as she did in "You Learn," she emphasizes that the cornerstone of any happiness or peace is the moment we choose to learn from our ghosts.

8

BEST FRIEND WITH BENEFITS

I think I was identifying as bisexual around the time I was arguing with my friends at school about whether Alanis was straight. My friends tried not to judge me for being some kind of queer, and I will never entirely shut the door on Alanis's not being heterosexual. The multiverse probably contains a bunch of parallel worlds where Alanis sometimes ends up queer and sometimes not, and somehow this particular self of mine ended up with a wife in one of the worlds where Alanis has a husband. When she admitted to some sexual experimentation in her younger years, I couldn't even muster up an "I told you so." My feelings about it amounted to nothing more than a quick nineties "duh" moment.

"Head over Feet" is responsible for my first and lasting impression that Alanis is essentially queer. It's the only love song on *JLP*, and there's no dude in it. Like so many of her lyrics, this song is addressed to "you," but unlike on other tracks this addressee has no gender, just the status of best friend getting elevated to a level with benefits. From the very first time I heard it, I felt the song truly charted what my experience of coming out would be like. I could not read the song any other way, and even though I had not yet had the pleasure of falling properly in love, "Head over Feet" was explaining to me how it would go. Out of survivalist necessity, there was a long time during which I avoided listening to my own feelings. Eventually, I had no choice but to come out because the prospect of being out of the closet seemed to involve less suffering than staying in. Being in the closet meant being alone instead of being in love.

Falling in love is necessarily part of the genre of coming-out stories because desire is only a hypothetical abstraction until we begin to feel something strong for someone and must decide whether to act on it or not. As I looked around for my first loves, I kept the checklist Alanis made for me: someone who will ask how my day was, someone who is braver than I initially give them credit for, someone who offers me unconditional things, someone who is patient, someone who seems healthy and rational. There must be some truth in this list, evidenced by one peculiar statistic: even though all five singles released in the US before this one had charted significantly, "Head over Feet" was Alanis's first single to land in the land of grownups on the *Billboard* Adult Top 40 list. Despite often getting in my own way, I did fall in love a handful of times based on these criteria for a healthy relationship. It was a big ask, because although of course I was worthy I was also a lot to handle—and vanity is the only thing causing me to put that line in the past tense instead of the present.

While I was falling in love with my future wife, Alanis was grieving the end of her engagement to Canadian actor Ryan Reynolds and drawing closer to beginning work on the material that would compose the *Flavors of Entanglement* album. Here again, we have Alanis failing beautifully at compulsory heterosexuality. The entire first half of the album criticizes the communication breakdown within a household, says this is at the root of why our world is at war, and points a finger at the man who won't accept his share of the blame. This guy is specifically Reynolds but is also an everyman extrapolation, its multiple versions of violence proliferating across the fragmentary yet highly danceable and organic sonic landscape composed of a cornucopia of synths, loops, and weird techno noises constructed by English producer Guy Sigsworth.

The second half of the album swears off men, commits to taking a break so the singer can find herself after vanquishing both outer and inner saboteurs, and grapples with having missed out on her own journey in trying to get to a destination that inherently cannot be reached. Regardless of who she desires, Alanis appears to process relationships queerly. Her instinctive sense of how to go about interpersonal communication and the importance of remaining aligned with her own values did not shift very much in the dozen years between *JLP* and *Flavors*. The optimistic vision of mutual support presented in "Head over Feet" still sounds like the right romance, tightly paralleling *Flavors* track number six of eleven, right there in the middle, "In Praise of the Vulnerable Man."

Both of these tracks express gratitude for a partner who is selfless and attentive, and they have a similar admiration for bravery. She may be a princess when she falls head over feet on *JLP*, but the maturation in evidence on *Flavors* turns this into a bow that evokes greater intentionality and a certain dignity. Here is a person who has learned to say no, and so giving her yes to the hypothetical future possibility of the vulnerable man is meant as a beautiful reward to them both. The alarm and surprise of loving in her younger days has been supplanted by the desire to give praise and say thank you to the person who can deliver the kind of loving that comes with more self-assuredness, the value of which we learned in chapter 7. "Head over Feet" describes the affirming efforts of a best friend while using language that playfully puts blame on that person for starting something extra good between them. "In Praise of the Vulnerable Man" employs a similar yin-yang pairing, using an extended war metaphor of the cavalry and its armor; it's a song about worshipping heroism that offers soft language for a tough guy: "You, with your new kind of heroism / And I bow and I bow down to you / To the grace that it takes to melt on through."

This track was the second single from *Flavors* to launch in the UK and Europe, yet it was given no real promotion and it failed to chart anywhere. I'm imagining a gaggle of male disc jockeys scratching their heads at the song title and ultimately shrugging off the song without giving it much of a listen. This is even though it's a more energetic and upbeat version of the *JLP* ballad that was such a smashing success. I wonder whether specifically gendering this vulnerability as a man's is what sunk the song. All the other songs on this album are gender-neutral, so that listeners can insert absolutely any person they want into the "you" spot. The one very amusing exception to this neutrality is that there are two references to God: one on "Not as We" that uses a masculine pronoun and one on "Incomplete" that uses a feminine pronoun.

So, I think we should claim her. Alanis is queer at least to the extent that she is a firm ally, consistently holding open the space for us to imagine ourselves in most of her lyrics without getting overwhelmed by feelings of gender dysphoria or body dysmorphia, and without much slippage into heteronormative presumptions about what a romance should be. In parallel with her queer thinking about interpersonal connection is the equally queer set of visual metaphors deployed in the music videos, not only in "Head over Feet" but in the campy coloration and jarringly unusual angles, cuts, and loops she has used in many subsequent videos over the years that push the boundaries of traditionally heteronormative narrative structures.

The first time Alanis directed her own video was for "Head over Feet," evocative of the "Nothing Compares 2 U" video for which Sinéad O'Connor won Video of the Year at the MTV Music Awards in 1990. The entire video is Alanis filling up the screen with her face as she sings. But she doesn't sing the entire time. The chorus most often plays without her lips moving, giving the impression that she's in dialogue with us as the audience to whom she is listening in those moments. At those times she looks down at her feet, while as she's singing she looks directly into the camera. She is breaking the fourth wall to connect directly and personally with the audience. It's both silly and skeptical, unsettling and intimate, these times when she has stopped singing but her gaze is still pointed at the camera. We know she is winking at us, campily provoking us into remembering that this is a lip sync, that the video isn't quite real.

The camera doesn't move and is focused for an extreme close-up against a pitch-black background. Whenever she moves around, sometimes to dance or to pick up her harmonica, she fades into the gloss of the background. This reminds us that we as viewers are in a fixed position. For us to see Alanis clearly, she must get right up close to us through the eye of the camera. She becomes blurry when physically backing away from us, at which point we no longer clearly see her facial expressions and thus can't follow the minutiae of her shifts in mood. Blurring the depth of field and sharpening the foreground creates an intimacy that Alanis can depressurize any time she wants by simply taking a step or two toward the background. It seems like she is vulnerable, but she's in the driver's seat.

It's a video that was done in one continuous take, although we don't know how many takes it took to get it just how she wanted. Such a thing is not easy to accomplish, as all the elements of the shoot must line up just right. The lighting had to be anticipatory of any movement, she had to be aware of the limits of the frame and the point at which she'd go from clear to blurry, the harmonica had to be off camera but close at hand, and so on. An unbroken video like this offers realism and immediacy to the audience. The unity and continuity of the performance immerses her audience in the performance of the song as if we were there in person. It's not a concert, but it utilizes one of the most intimate aspects of the concertgoing experience, which is the feeling that we're all experiencing the same thing at the same time.

She's wearing very little makeup in this video, just some neutral shade of lipstick and a small flush of color on her cheeks. The few times we see more than an inch below her chin, we notice black and white tank top straps that also somewhat blend with the black background. The overall effect of this black and white look, or perhaps black and beige, is that Alanis is unadorned and unarmored, not dripping with the usual music video trappings but instead stripped down and giving us her naked thoughts and feelings. This again creates a feeling of intimacy with the audience, as if she's just being herself in earnest and not trying to impress anyone with an over-the-top performance.

Each of these queer intimacies can be seen in her subsequent video work, too. Nonlinear narratives, used to convey the complexity and fluidity of queer lives, are found in the video for the *Flavors of Entanglement* track "Underneath," where there is an inner world depicted alongside an outer world. These two stories are told on parallel tracks as the audience swings back and forth between them. A related technique is the split-screening of the story told by the video for "Precious Illusions," from the *Under Rug Swept* album, showing a real-life romance on one side and a fairytale romance on the other. There is also a dreamy, disjointed sequence of events in the video for *JLP*'s "You Learn."

The blurring technique was used to great effect in "Hand in My Pocket," with Alanis ever in focus as the rest of humanity streams by in a parade all around her. It was used also for the iconic "Thank U" video from *Supposed Former Infatuation Junkie*, as Alanis walks down the streets of a city completely naked to convey themes of personal empowerment and self-acceptance. Videos from the *Havoc and Bright Lights* album, for "Guardian" and "Receive," both go from a black and white palette to a vibrantly colorful one when they depict the sudden clarity of resolution and overcoming of obstacles in their stories. And she plays a half dozen characters who all campily break the fourth wall as the camera round-robins across their support group circle in the video for "Reasons I Drink" from the *Such Pretty Forks in the Road* album.

When she looks directly at me, I feel seen as I am and as

I could be, in the best possible way. In her nakedness and intimacy, she is supportive of our queer emotional states. She reminds us we can blur the background and focus on our own well-being. I don't have to paint my face to femme it up or else choose to act manly about stuff to fit into the world she's creating. Her music and videos have been non-toxic for my kind. I am in love with Alanis not as a prospect for romantic partnership but as an ally who can be counted upon to consistently create space for me in my attempts at being my best and queerest self.

9

LOSING WEIGHT AGAIN

"Mary Jane" is one of the only third-person narrations on the *JLP* album, perhaps because Alanis wanted just a little distance between herself and its issues even though each character on the album ultimately reflects facets of her own sense of self. Alanis has been relatively open about her addictions to overeating, starving, binging, and purging over the years. Food is necessary and medicinal, yet for those who face challenges with eating, it can be difficult to understand what recovery should look like.

The lyrics to "Mary Jane" make the mental health messaging quite plain. MJ's life is full of the usual derailments, and she is coping "again" by losing weight. With awful irony, her burden grows heavier as she gets thinner: "I hear you're losing weight again, Mary Jane / Ever wonder who you're losing it for?" The song provides definitions of freedom and safety, presents a hierarchy of needs, and advocates for doing something rather than acquiescing to wasting away: "So take this moment Mary Jane and be selfish / Worry not about the cars that go by / Cause all that matters Mary Jane is your freedom." The chorus exhorts her to be honest about her cycles of unhappiness and to be more self-interested in setting boundaries that can provide some real comfort whenever she might need it.

The Mary Jane character recurs as the protagonist in the

Broadway musical version of *JLP*, which debuted at the Broadhurst Theatre in 2019, directed by Diane Paulus with a book by Diablo Cody. It won a Tony for Best Musical Book and a Grammy for Best Musical Theater Album. In the story told by the musical, which I had the good fortune to see for myself on December 3, 2021, we see the evolution of a young girl struggling with food into a fully grown adult with an opioid addiction, who must repeatedly learn not to avoid or suppress the challenges presented by her own mental health. In the Christmas letter opener dictated aloud to introduce the family in the musical, MJ exclaims, "It's amazing what you can get used to with a little discipline!" She is referring literally to hot yoga, but this is a campy way of saying that also, in a larger sense, she has disciplined herself into feeling nothing.

Cody says in the musical book that "Mary Jane" was the hinge song from *JLP* on which her entire sense of the musical's plot was constructed. "If that song wasn't on *Jagged Little Pill*," Cody insists, "I couldn't begin to tell you what the show would be about. Because that was the beginning of all of it and it wound up informing the entire production." In the musical book, MJ is described as a "good Catholic girl, devoted wife, Harvard mom, PTA president, SoulCycle star, Trader Joe's shopper, Christmas letter writer, control freak, car accident victim, opioid addict, rape survivor." A car accident triggers in her the resurgence of traumatic feelings about being assaulted in college. Even MJ's husband, Steve, doesn't know this happened, let alone that she's been turning to a drug dealer since her prescription for painkillers ran out.

The musical book offers a bunch of little inserts to create ambiance and give a sense of the characters. MJ's birthday is listed on the rehab intake form as 5/15/74—Alanis's own birthday is 6/1/74. "Mary Jane" is the seventh of nine songs in Act 2, but of course it's sung to her rather than by her. It's interesting how the construction of an MJ character for the musical necessarily gives additional agency to this portion of Alanis's self-concept while also advancing this facet of it to connect with other songs from her catalog in a way that the original *JLP* album could not. Director Paulus says in the musical book, "It's not accidental that we're making this show now, when we're more in touch with Alanis who has lived a life. We're not frozen in time when Alanis was nineteen. We're in this dynamic living relationship with everything that Alanis has channeled and learned and is living today."

With time comes experience, and experience begets wisdom. First, there are some cool changes to the lyrics. When MJ and her daughter Frankie fight by singing "All I Really Want" at each other, they sub in "your pills" for "your bills" in the line "your bills, your ex, your deadlines." In this case, it just happens to jive nicely with an essential plot point, demonstrating that Alanis and her crew viewed even relatively sacred lines from the songs as fair game for reinterpretation based on the storyline. They did not simply cram as much story as they could into an inflexible jukebox of her original hit singles.

Frankie also changes the lyrics to be "fascinated by a spiritual woman" instead of a man. This example demonstrates exactly what Paulus said about the fact that we cannot freeze our total understanding of Alanis in the moment when we first apprehended her nineteen-year-old self. She has lived and learned, and the "spiritual woman" line is actually one that she has been singing live for about a decade now. The audiences go nuts when she does it in concert, so she updated the lyrics for the musical to match, and the Broadway audience likewise loves it.

Mary Jane's solo song in Act 1 is "Smiling," which Alanis wrote for the musical and subsequently released as the first single for the *Such Pretty Forks* album. During the song, MJ is moving backward through time, engaged in reliving her usual routine and all the little elements that make up her morning. The choreography for "Smiling" is truly rigorous in that the characters first have to move through MJ's day, then reverse every movement. It was the most-rehearsed number for the show. MJ sings "Me the ceilingless great achiever / Me the notorious perfect mother." On the album, it's "Me, the notorious bottom dweller / Me, the ceilingless brave explorer." Fortysomething Alanis can carve out space to be humble, while MJ is still attached to pressures belonging to the teenage Alanis.

Composer Tom Kitt says in the musical book that he "added a backing choir so it felt like MJ was praying. The arrangement gives the character's pain and defense mechanisms a bit of a holy place." It's a song about fighting to keep up appearances even as the perfectionist demands of living a boring suburban life threaten to overwhelm MJ, who is both happy and struggling. Of this ambivalence, Alanis says in the musical book, "My friends can't read me because I have a tendency to present as smiling. But for me, that's just because I want to get the job done. It's very masculine too. It's not just because of the patriarchy, it's also because I'm super androgynous and I love to get stuff done. It's a mature muscle, I think." Please go ahead and add that quotation to the evidentiary pile of queer tidbits from our previous chapters. Elizabeth Stanley, who originated the role of MJ in the show, says in the musical book that the character's conflicting positive and negative feelings offer a "wild juxtaposition" very much in keeping with the vibe of the nineties that we examined in chapter 4.

The only way to settle such tension is by honesty, as recommended in the "Mary Jane" lyrics, but MJ isn't ready. Her initial reaction to the possibility that her son's friend Bella was raped at a party is to downplay and dismiss it by saying, "A girl got drunk and someone took advantage of her. It's a shame but it happens all the time." That's MJ's own story, which she has relied upon to suppress her trauma for so long. When MJ tries to tell Bella that "bad things happen. And we have to be strong and accept our mistakes and move on," Bella claps back with "tell me when I'm going to feel normal again." Then both suddenly realize they will never feel "normal" again.

MJ singing "Forgiven" ends up proving our earlier point in chapter 6 about the real lesson of that song: she must first give grace to herself. In this scene, she's still asking God for an assist. The end of the song blends together with some phrases from "Ave Maria." The church is empty, but when MJ walks out, her drug dealer rolls by and dispenses the pills into her hand, fulfilling the role of her priest. This is the first time she's really acknowledged that what happened to her was rape. In a footnote to "Forgiven" in the musical book, Alanis says, "I would describe myself as a little obsessed with religion. There's a thread of continuity that permeates through all religions. There's always something about connectivity, humility, prayer, and ritual."

Everyone in Alanis's musical audience is there for a jagged little worship, though not everyone there has experience with opioid addiction or rape. The book for the musical includes educational materials for four of the main challenges addressed within the story. There are two "Facing the Facts" inserts per act: in Act 1, for LGBTQ identity and opioid addiction; in Act 2, for transracial adoption and sexual assault. This info is bleakly presented in white text on a black background, as many of Alanis's communications are. But these are fact sheets, not personal letters from her about the issues. Disappointingly, only the fact sheet on transracial adoption provides a brief resource list, and there are no calls to action accompanying all the scary stats.

In her introduction to the book, Alanis says that she wanted the musical to challenge her sense of activism and push her to give back. During the early pandemic lockdown, she got together with the cast members on Zoom and sang with them as a benefit for the Actor's Fund. The "Facing the Facts" page on opioid addiction cites the nonprofit addiction support network Learn to Cope, which also provided resources and stories directly to aid in the cast's understanding of what MJ would be going through. Of the heavy violence and abuse topics in the show, Alanis says in the musical book, "I mean it's all over a lot of my songs, it's all over my history. And it's all over most fucking women's history. People say one in five women have been assaulted. I'm like, *every* woman's been subject to some version, covert or overt, of sexual harassment, abuse. Even just being a woman in a body you're going to be subject to something."

Paulus also agreed to give up ten hours of rehearsal time to train the entire cast plus crew and support staff on sensitive topics addressed by the show. Her overall reaction to the intersection of these issues is that they are even clearer and timelier now. Paulus says in the musical book that "Diablo was asking, 'Is it too many issues?' But we just kept working on it and feeling it was interesting, and all the issues that were coming felt like they were threaded and relevant. [. . .] And every young person I talked to said, 'This is what we're navigating. These are all the issues that are present concurrently in our lives.'"

The graphics toward the end of the book show a Sunday services pamphlet from St. Mary Mother of Sorrows Parish, listing MJ's new nonprofit, the Serenity Café, a coffee shop in a local shopping center that aims to help women in recovery from addictions by employing them. By the time MJ is in recovery at the end of the musical, she is more able to reflect the thinking of the fortysomething Alanis, including seeking support for topical nonprofits and charitable endeavors.

Alanis has been involved with a cornucopia of well-known causes over the years, including Stand Up to Cancer, People for the Ethical Treatment of Animals, RAINN, and Greenpeace. She also sponsors children through World Vision, a Christian humanitarian organization that combats poverty, hunger, and injustice. Additionally, she has supported StandWithUs, to educate people of all ages about anti-Semitism and anti-Israel bias; the Lunchbox Fund, which provides daily meals to kids in South Africa; and Bono's ONE Campaign, to end extreme poverty and preventable diseases.

Alanis told Rachel Syme, who wrote the foreword for the musical book, that the musical "was supposed to feel like a deluge, much in the way that her original album feels like a forceful weather pattern." Syme concludes that "the show is too much, but that is no longer something to be feared" because learning doesn't always have a slow pace or a linearity to help us feel comfortable with change. The musical is thus deliberately inconclusive. It ends on a note of catharsis, not resolution. Celia Rose Gooding, who originated the role of Frankie in the musical, says of the ending, "I think one of the morals of the show is, you have to help yourself before you can help somebody else. One of the beautiful things about our show was that there really is no concrete solution. There's just constant improvement and you can only try to be the best person you can be and support those around you the best you can." Alanis told Syme "many times" that her main goal is "open communication above all things," and Syme agrees the musical embodies that goal by depicting a family whose conflicts stem mainly from not being honest with themselves or each other.

Gooding reflects in the musical book that "so much of that [need for honesty] was communicated from Alanis herself. I think that's where Alanis is, in every moment when someone tells the truth for the first time." Anyone can tell the truth for the first time, but delivering Alanis's truth might be highly gendered. There are two main male characters in the show: MJ's husband, Steve, and their son, Nick. Steve gets to start "So Unsexy," which then shifts into a duet with MJ. Nick gets to sing "Perfect." We should consider what it means for these songs to be sung by men, instead of by Alanis. Cody speculates, "I do think of Alanis as such a specifically feminine artist. She's such a goddess. But I think the material translates."

Cody goes on to say that using Steve's voice adds another level of heartbreak to "So Unsexy." For Steve to sing "Not the Doctor" in a duet with MJ, the lyrics had to be changed from "I don't want to be adored for what I merely represent to you / I don't want to be your babysitter / You're a very big boy now" to "I don't want to be resented when I'm just trying to provide for you / I don't want to be berated for simply doing my best to reach you." Alanis also enjoys the contributions of Steve's perspective. When MJ and Steve have an awkward first couples therapy session, Alanis remarks in a footnote for the musical book, "I love this moment when MJ makes this acerbic and cynical comment, and Steve responds by saying, 'See, she's funny.' It's so sweet. This is one of my favorite scenes. Working with Diablo, I based it on my own experience being a psychotherapeutic girl."

When Steve begins to sing "Mary Jane" in Act 2, Scene 7, MJ is unconscious in her hospital bed recovering from the overdose. Steve is offering the song as a serenade or lullaby, evoking peace and protection in a way that is bound to feel different from the album version of "Mary Jane," which portrays two women helping each other through their common understandings as women. Alanis says in the musical book, "This song is just an opportunity to be intensely empathic. It's saying: 'I see you. I hear you.' It's the most beautiful thing for me to hear empathic words coming out of a male voice." The sisterhood messaging of the original track is lost, but we've gained the musical's ideal of the vulnerable man that we began to envision in chapter 8. I'll bet some of the men who felt attacked by *JLP* in the nineties will find relief and clarity in the inclusive approach of the musical.

10

YEAH, I REALLY DO THINK

Who knows where I was when I first realized that X is impossible without the idea of not-X, when it suddenly dawned on me that any given word or event contains both the expectation and its opposite? Except that I will guarantee I was in some advanced English course, as most of the significant intellectual growth spurts in my young life occurred either in lit classes or at debate tournaments. From debate, I got that there are at least two sides to every idea, and from lit, I got that all sides collapse into each other until the only thing left is an existential anxiety about the violence of the unknown. That's the essential vibe of the nineties teenage climate, wherein the definitive literary concept manifesting in the culture was irony.

You know where this is headed. The prevailing notion is that the song "Ironic" is not ironic at all, but instead simply full of bummers. This is a pedantic and sad case of unimaginative people wielding sexist bias to dismiss Alanis as dumb. Alanis has admitted that the lyrics to "Ironic" prove she didn't properly grasp the meaning of the word. We're not here to rehash verdicts already rendered. She fucked it up and said so. We're here to examine the implications of that fuck up, to explain why it was usefully so very on the nose for the nineties and to argue that the song is redeemable while the critique of it is not.

The commonly understood definition of irony, where what is said is literally the opposite of what is meant, comes to us from Greek philosophers. This is verbal irony, or in nineties parlance, sarcasm. It's saying, "Oh, yay, I get to flunk another math test this week," when what you mean is that you are freaked out about your consistently terrible grades in math class. Situational irony is when what happens is the opposite of what is expected to happen. It's when you somehow get an A on that math test despite being utterly unprepared for it. Sometimes, the math teacher acknowledges situational irony by asking you to stay after class so he can accuse you of cheating, since neither of you can believe you suddenly aced a test by any other method.

By the measure of the Greeks, the song "Ironic" is a technical failure because it serves bummers in lieu of true opposites. Yet Alanis is far from dumb, and a case-by-case nitpicking of the lines is as micro as Socrates playing devil's advocate in response to every little thing his students say, while the song is operating at a macro or meta level more akin to Aristotle's notion of infinite regress. The fable goes that someone asks what holds up the earth in space and is told the planet rests on the back of a giant turtle. So, the question then is what that giant turtle rests on, and the answer of course is another giant turtle. It's turtles all the way down into the abyss. Alanis is interested in these mystic "slippery slope" moments, these big-ticket human crises that feel apocalyptic yet idiotic. She didn't spend any time checking whether the chardonnay or Mr. Play It Safe were properly aligned with the rules of irony. No admiration from Socrates then, but perhaps plenty from Aristotle.

We don't know whether Alanis read or cared about the Greeks, but she's made hundreds of mentions of Swiss psychoanalyst Carl Jung and how his pioneering theories of analytical psychology deeply influence her songwriting. Jung died in the early sixties before irony began trending as a fundamental human relation. Although he had no explicit definition of irony, he theorized that humans are strongly influenced by symbols expressed through myths and dreams or other cultural touchstones. In his emphasis on the gap between our surface words or actions and their deeper psychological meanings or feelings, Jung would probably say that irony questions and subverts normative cultural narratives. He would understand irony as an archetype drawn from our collective unconscious.

This is the way in to grasping how Alanis *does* effectively utilize irony. She has a deep understanding of and a postmodern comfort with cognitive dissonance, with lyrics that describe the affective landscape of the gap between our gestures and expectations. Sadly, one of the best defenses of "Ironic" comes to us from Vince Vaughn. The opening sequence of the 2013 film *The Internship*, which Vaughn wrote and starred in, has "Ironic" blasting in a convertible with the top down as Vaughn and Owen Wilson head out for a night on the town. Wilson is dismayed that this song is on Vaughn's "get psyched" playlist and they debate it. "I defy you to crush this chorus and not get psyched," Vaughn says. Wilson does so and then is indeed psyched. One hundred percent of the examples given in "Ironic" are bummers, and yet the lyrics close with a reminder that life has a funny way of helping you out.

That's Barthesian irony. Roland Barthes was a French literary critic who worked in semiotics, the study of signs and symbols, just as Jung did. Compared to the Greeks' understanding of it, Barthesian irony is less concerned with opposites. He simply defined it as a rhetorical device involving a double meaning. The discrepancy between the two meanings generates ambiguity and this ambiguity can push a listener to interpret the lyrics of "Ironic" in a new way. You can sing about all the bummers in "Ironic," but do so joyfully, embracing even the hard parts of life as inevitable or necessary. Our struggles help us out. Framing something bad as somehow yielding something good is a subversive move when it allows multiple, conflicting interpretations of a song at the same time. It offers ten thousand spoons instead of one knife. This multiplication of meaning is a form of linguistic play, a turning to imagine what one might do with the unexpected bounty of ten thousand spoons. When critics dismiss "Ironic" as made up of a failed set of literal opposites, they miss the point: irony is a rhetorical whirlwind that disrupts language and undermines normativity.

Dualistic dismissals of "Ironic" foreclose its vivacious, nonbinary complexity. "Irony does not involve the simple substitution of the opposite for the literal meaning," said Barthes in *Elements of Semiology*. "It is a form of semantic pivot which overturns the hierarchy of language, bringing into play the signified and the signifier, the explicit and the implicit, the internal and the external, the present and the absent." By Barthesian standards, "Ironic" is ironic. This is especially true when Alanis questions whether life can be a little too ironic. The Greeks conceived of irony as pass/fail, but Alanis considers irony to be a spectrum, and she slides from side to side across the examples in the song in a manner that is definitely akin to Barthesian play.

The most critics can really claim is that she didn't do so on purpose.

To the extent that her intentions are discernible, I agree that they should matter to our discussion here. Barthes expects irony to be done deliberately. Fortunately, life does seem to have a funny way of helping Alanis out. After she realized her erroneous deployment of the concept, she was given a shot at redemption in the opportunity to carefully consider how to position "Ironic" in the *Jagged Little Pill* Broadway musical. This was an epic chance to reject, remedy, or advance criticisms of the original album. Older and wiser Alanis did not throw the moment away, but instead positioned the critique itself within the musical to add further layers of irony. The plot of the musical updates the context of the lyrics by putting them into a writing workshop as a poem, with other characters criticizing the poem's lack of irony.

"Ironic" is the fifth of ten songs in Act 1, and its beautiful reversal hunts the hunters. It laughs them right off the stage, not meanly or defensively—because they are somewhat correct about the lack of opposites in the song—but instead with a disregard for any criticism that would tend to deny the overall gorgeousness of the poem on the basis of a technicality. Rachel Syme's foreword to the musical book says that this version of "Ironic" turns it into "an inside joke about poetic license and grammatical errors." The song and the scene are given to Frankie, described in the musical book as an "aspiring poet, president and founder of SMAAC (The Social Movements and Advocacy Committee), proud Black woman, bisexual feminist, perennial troublemaker, revolutionary in the making." She's also adopted. SMAAC only has two members at first,

Frankie and her best friend/girlfriend, Jo. Frankie makes mistakes but is also a strong advocate for others.

The Writer's Workshop classroom at Frankie's high school is found in Act 1, Scene 5. The teacher says, "Frankie will read her piece and we will then use constructive criticism to help her shape it into something brilliant-ish." Frankie describes her writing, the lyrics to "Ironic," as "an essay-poem-story-type" thing. After the first verse, Alanis included a footnote in the musical book stating, "I get it when people mock these lyrics. The real irony of all time for me is that I'm usually the grammar police. I'm usually the one going, 'Ah, that's not the King's English.'" In the musical, one classmate interrupts Frankie to say, "That's not irony, that's just, like, shitty." Another classmate says it fails according to the definition of irony present in Greek tragedy. One more classmate tries to improve upon the plane crash scenario with the old man, to make it actually ironic by turning him into an airplane mechanic instead of a guy who was afraid to fly. Frankie's love interest, Phoenix, consoles her by saying these critics are projecting, that Frankie is "obviously a great writer and their only defense is to be hyperliteral." With renewed confidence, Frankie continues to sing as Phoenix duets on the remaining verses.

In this version of "Ironic," Frankie sings, "It's like meeting the boy of my dreams and then meeting his . . ." Phoenix finishes the line with ". . . I'm not seeing anyone." The album finishes it with ". . . beautiful wife." The last time I saw Alanis live, she finished it with ". . . beautiful husband," making it explicitly queer and generating extra cheers from the crowd. She left a footnote here in the musical book: "For the last eight years or so, whenever I perform it in concert, I sing 'Meeting the man of my dreams

/ And then meeting his beautiful husband.' Which is true. I have fallen in love with a lot of gay men." Again, I'm just obligated here, as a sidebar, to keep flagging instances of Alanis being an ally to my people.

Diablo Cody knew she wanted to directly address the decades of controversy about "Ironic," especially given that Alanis consistently has a playful attitude about the criticism. Cody writes that Alanis was "always open" to poking gentle fun at the song and "there is such a discourse around the inaccuracy of that song." The use of "inaccuracy" here is telling, as if a rhetorical device could be objectively correct or not. She set the debate in an English class because it absolutely does belong there. "I would not have taken that meta approach unless I had felt that the song demanded it," she wrote. Rather than make fun of the song, Cody forthrightly admits she wanted to "make fun of the song's critics."

Celia Rose Gooding relates to the way criticism is deployed against her character, to shut her up in a grand sense just as critics tried to quiet Alanis. "People don't like it when women speak their truth," Gooding says in the musical book. "When you can find a little piece of something almost fractionally incorrect, it's so easy to just say, 'You're wrong. You're stupid. You don't know what you're talking about, girl.'" There's the feminist seedling. We've covered why the broader French mode of irony that makes space for "Ironic" is superior to the Greek mode that excludes it, but we have not yet tied the irony issue to a larger conversation about sexism in the dismissal of Alanis's work.

For this, we turn to the work of Lauren Berlant. Berlant was one of the most influential twenty-first-century

American cultural critics, known for pioneering the field of affect studies. Though they didn't build upon Jung directly, their examination of how emotions are socially constructed is well aligned with Jung's notion of how archetypes format human experience. Berlant theorizes that women's feelings are simultaneously expressed and constrained by sentimentality. The portrayal of intense emotional states tied to women's experiences is certainly a main mission of Alanis's body of work and could also be considered a Jungian archetype. *JLP* is exemplary of the psychological landscaping Berlant is interested in as a cultural expression operating at the intersection of emotion, gender, and power in public life. To silo or deride the mission of Alanis is to file it away as "female complaint."

In Berlant's view, irony is a key mode of expression in contemporary life because it showcases the gap between our ideals and the reality of our lived experience. It's like meeting the man of your dreams and then meeting his beautiful husband. Irony produces laughs and shrugs that help us navigate the emotional and political contradictions of everyday life. Because women are often marginalized or excluded from dominant cultural narratives, irony provides us a means to subvert them and a pressure-release valve for our ambivalence about whether transformative social change is possible. "Ironic" shows how our expectations are consistently defeated by life, yet we do get psyched when we sing it. Berlant coined the term "juxtapolitical" to describe this messy, contradictory tangle of social and emotional interconnectedness that reveals itself as we grapple with our multidimensional context, using archetypes like the bummer situations presented in the lyrics of "Ironic."

On top of this endorsement of irony, Berlant also theorized a post-irony characterized by meaningful sincerity, allowing us to patch or bridge the affective conflicts of public life that can't be resolved through ironic detachment. They were a "both-and" kind of theorist, just as Alanis is. Berlant thought that marginalized groups can't afford the cruel optimism of attaching to unattainable happily-ever-after narratives, even if these American dream fantasies continue to shape culture. Between Barthes and Berlant, Alanis gets to have the black fly in her chardonnay and drink it, too. The worst-case scenario for "Ironic" here turns out to be not that bad at all. Alanis was both behind her times and ahead of them: behind in the sense that she may have botched one interpretation of irony, but ahead in the sense that her sincerity and authenticity were harbingers of a post-ironic future. In oscillating between expressing radical emotional honesty and playing with failure in her utilization of irony, she served up a prophetic glimpse of what ultimately became the standard milieu of young people at the crossroads between irony-obsessed Millennials and sincerity-possessed Gen Zers.

Here's a quick example of how young people still get Alanis while critical oldsters fail to learn any new tricks. In 2005, a decade after *JLP*, the Black Eyed Peas released a song called "My Humps," which Alanis subsequently covered ironically. She was offering a critique, a feminist rejection of the supposedly postfeminist objectification of Fergie's hot body. The video Alanis made for it shows her elbowing a handsy dude in the face. She also slowed the tempo way down to give it a less danceable ballad vibe. Her cover went massively viral and young people briefly allowed it to rule the internet because they totally understood the "both-and" of it, while those with some journalistic power often did not. Of the fact that it is still normal for Alanis to be criticized in this way, all I can say is it figures. Some descriptions of the "My Humps" cover from male critics: not funny, smug, witless, self-conscious, pop music cannibalism, dreadful, and completely missing the point. Personally—and ironically—I'm more comfortable assigning those descriptions to her critics.

11

IF THE WOUND IS NOT MINE

"Not the Doctor" has probably been paid less attention than any other track on *JLP*. It wasn't released as a single, no video was made for it, most reviewers don't mention it, biographers tend to zoom out in favor of bigger hits, there are no diehard fans doing long homages to it on their personal blogs, nobody lip syncs to it on social media, et cetera. Personally, I've always felt this song simmering usefully in the background and now with hindsight I can see how it points toward Alanis's sense of her own legacy and celebrity, even if it was originally written to slough off a boyfriend who wanted her to be his therapist.

It is an incantation of refusal. "Not the Doctor" is an outlier on *JLP* because it says no. Saying "no": what a thrilling prospect to fifteen-year-old me when I first fully grasped it! The album's other songs are largely invitations to make connection, not to sever it as we see here. The other songs solicit or provoke dialogue, whereas this one defines what is unwelcome. It's not about duality or paradox as so many of her songs are. The message is uncomplicated at this decision stage. She is not prepared to take on the anxious responsibility of solving other people's problems, and stacks up metaphors for this type of emotional labor in a complex "I don't wanna" anaphora series that resembles Lloyd Dobler's goal-oriented dinner table speech in Cameron Crowe's 1989 cult classic film *Say Anything*. Played by John Cusack, Lloyd meets his girlfriend's parents and they inquire about his future plans. He stuns them with a few thoughtfully poetic lines: "I don't want to sell anything, buy anything or process anything as a career. I don't want to sell anything bought or processed, or buy anything sold or processed, or . . . process anything sold, bought or processed, or repair anything sold, bought or processed, you know, as a career I don't want to do that."

Both Cusack's speech and the "Not the Doctor" lyrics share the use of anaphora with the repetition of "I don't want to," but there are additional similarities beyond the literal. Both the speech and the song are an assertion of personal boundaries. These two people refuse to conform to societal expectations and pursue a conventional path, to fulfill the traditional role of being someone's emotional caretaker or savior. That defiance of societal pressures in favor of personal autonomy and agency highlights the power of their individual choices. They're both examples of emotional independence and self-reliance.

These refusals eliminate a lot of possibilities by preventing certain forms of engagement, which some might critique as an inconveniently narrow or unnecessarily rigid way of dealing with the burden of other people's existence. Alanis chooses to set a tough boundary, declining the responsibility of fixing someone else with the implication that helping him so substantively would require her to toss aside her own self-care. This is a bit of a riff on Sartre's idea that hell is other people, as Alanis firmly argues that other people are not a cure for whatever ails you—or that even if they could be the cure, they shouldn't want to be. This notion goes well past the one-on-one drama of a romantic relationship, working toward the relationship between an artist and her fans.

We can debate the extent of her fame's ebb and flow in any given window of time, but Alanis is inarguably a celebrity. All celebrities engage in forms of emotional labor to support their fans, whether because it's profitable or because they genuinely care to do so. A celebrity puts on a good show, graciously signs autographs and answers fan mail, fights to keep prices accessible for their products, gives organized attention to causes that are in the orbit of their interests, and so on. There are reasons why being a celebrity is hard work and one of the main reasons is that the relationship is usually pretty one-sided. These are parasocial relationships, in which fans believe they know so much about every little detail of Alanis's life and values that they are comfortable viewing her as a close friend even though most of them have not even properly met her, let alone established a genuine, ongoing exchange with her.

There's an Alanis tribute band in New York City called Not the Doctor. Within parasocialism, a gray area that has always fascinated me is the nature of covers and tribute bands, which we touched on in chapter 4. Alanis has been steadfastly in favor of covers and tribute bands, saying both that she's honored by them and that she values the community created by them. Not the Doctor has been around since at least 2015 and they have about four hundred followers on Facebook. They mostly pop up as an opening act to play the *JLP* album in full at nineties nostalgia events, and they don't appear to be covering any of her subsequent albums. They're okay if you've had a couple of beers.

There's an Italian equivalent of that group, with half as many followers, who call themselves the Ironic Band.

Their lead singer wears knee-length skirts and high heels at shows, even though I'm pretty sure Alanis has never, ever performed in either of those, which opens up a can of authenticity worms. Alaniz Morizzette, a truly great band in the Netherlands, has a lead singer who can mimic nearly all the album vocals but opts instead for her own interestingly melodic adaptations of them, and perhaps more importantly looks and moves eerily like Alanis. We have Alani in Los Angeles and Alanis Unplugged in New York. We have You Oughta Know in Canada, of course. The UK has The Jagged Little Band and Australia has Jagged Little Pill. This is not even remotely an exhaustive list, but it already leaves me wondering why a group of people would form a band whose mission is to glorify a single album by a single artist through their occasional performance of it. The depth of love and corresponding study is surely intense, and in some sense it does make Alanis the doctor even when she is wholly unaware of the existence or activities of a specific tribute band.

Performing in a tribute band seems to grant several healing powers. Most obviously, it creates community and a sense of belonging for the band and their audience by calling Alanis fans together to celebrate their common fandom. In an even more deeply emotive sense, it can provide catharsis. If *JLP* holds personal significance for us as the soundtrack to whatever was going on with us during the mid-nineties portion of our lives, performing that album now is a way to process and release some of the trauma from those times. Third, it appears to provide a sense of purpose or fulfillment by bringing accessible joy to the audience. The cost of a front row seat to see Alanis herself is usually a three or four-digit number, while the cost of a front row seat at the local bar to see any of these tribute bands is unlikely to cost more than twenty bucks.

Even the *JLP* Broadway show is technically two hours of covers, and Alanis worked hard to make that happen, so tributes must feel valuable to her in some way. These bands provide validation and affirmation for her artistic output by prolonging the echo of the original work in their own performances. This helps to keep her work alive and relevant and extends her legacy, especially when it introduces her to younger generations that were born after 1995. Hopefully she gets some joy herself out of listening to other bands perform the album with skill or at least with passion. Perhaps she wishes that these bands would play some of her other hits or maybe an occasional B-side, and yet covering the entire *JLP* album means you do get songs like "Not the Doctor" in circulation even if that's the song where everyone breaks for the restroom or grabs their last drink for the night.

There's also the chance for collaboration or inspiration, as some of these tribute bands might offer Alanis fresh insights into her own music or even be a bridge to relationships with other artists. She may have learned the value here from putting together the Broadway show, as her next project included an extended-play remix album, which she had never done before. She has often remixed a hit single from an album but has never gathered together a bunch of musicians to remix most of an album. After the July 2020 launch of *Such Pretty Forks in the Road* from Epiphany, she collaborated with Thirty Tigers and He.She.They. Records to launch *Such Pretty Forks in the Mix* in December 2020. The album spotlights six trans-inclusive female musicians plus two live acoustic performances of "Smiling" and

"Reasons I Drink" from her March 2020 show in London. The remix album was a fundraiser for Safe Place International, whose mission is to provide safety, community, and support systems for queer refugees. In the case of this album, the funds went to LGBTQ+ refugees in Greece and Turkey.

Emotional labor is embedded in all the facets of *Such Pretty Forks* and its remix album. Like any celebrity, Alanis must steer the crafting of her public image so that she can connect with fans, while also handling inevitable criticisms and backlash from the media or the public, exponentially multiplied now by the echo chamber of the internet. All of this requires Alanis to regulate her emotions so that she can provide support to her fans through speaking out on social issues, sharing aspects of her personal life and thoughts with them and offering them encouraging words. She describes both the honor of and the taxing nature of this work on *Such Pretty Forks*, which is literally about motherhood and her two kids but figuratively just as much about mothering her art and her fans.

In "Not the Doctor," Alanis proposes that life is a steady stream of if-then statements to be negotiated head-on, and this is a theory of how best to live one's life that is still very much in evidence on *Such Pretty Forks*, whose title is itself evocative of the opportunity cost of our choices about boundaries. Consider the material she was steeped in when she began writing this album in 2017. Across twenty-one episodes of the *Conversation with Alanis Morissette* podcast, which ran from October 2015 through December 2018, literally all the guests are psychologists. Most of them have written psychology or self-help books, a lot of them are academics or in private practices, and a handful of them run nonprofits or lead research think tanks. The anchoring theme of these podcasts is relationship maintenance generally and attachment theory specifically. The central tenet of attachment theory is that kids need the stability of a relationship with at least one primary caregiver to have healthy development socially and emotionally. It's not a very contestable point, but there is debate about how best to put the idea into practice.

In this public study on how best to raise her kids, Alanis is extending attachment theory as a metaphor for her relationship to her fans. As the album's lyrics make clear, there is an element of letting go in both kinds of mothering. When we take one path, we don't get to know what would've happened if we had taken the other path at the fork. If the healthy flexibility and optimism of *Such Pretty Forks* seems kind of uncool compared to the direct obstinance of *JLP*, that's probably because older and wiser Alanis knows it gets exhausting to try to control everything, that it is braver to simply exist in the present moment with another person and embrace the path you find yourself on now without regret. Kids are going to be kids and fans are going to be fans, and neither of them really knows what prices Alanis has been willing to pay for these relationships. She wants to keep the lights in our eyes ablaze even though we don't know that it might be too much to ask for.

Such Pretty Forks won the Adult Contemporary Album of the Year Award at the 2021 Juno Awards. Of course, it must please Alanis to receive this validation of her emotional labor, and yet in another equally very real sense she must not care too much about that. Literally every album Alanis has made has been called "the best album she's made since *Jagged Little Pill*" by more than a handful of reviewers, and only time will tell whether the newly formed semi-consensus among them that *Such Pretty Forks* is indeed the best since *JLP* will hold. It's been called the album with the strongest thematic likeness to, and the one musically closest to, *JLP*. It's been called a proper and comparable follow-up and a true successor. It's been called a return to her confessionalist approach, as if she has ever paused in pioneering that spirit mode. Her fans and her children can vouch for Alanis always having been there.

12

NO AMOUNT OF MY INSISTENCE

For a long while, I assumed that my teenage self would consider my adult self a sellout. After two decades of working with teenagers, which in many ways trapped me at the crime scene of my own high school traumas, eventually I woke up and began to heal. Wokeness has additional meaning in modern slang that it didn't have when Alanis wrote "Wake Up," and it's a good surprise to see how the shoe still fits. Today, to be woke means an individual is socially and politically aware of the trials and tribulations associated with identity politics. Inequality and systemic injustice were also hot topics for me during the nineties. At fifteen, I was intensely critical of every facet of the mainstream narrative, already feeling sure that the dominant cultural norms were designed to exclude and oppress me, that the system's values were not mine. Nirvana's Kurt Cobain destined me for a life of ice-skating uphill when he told *Rolling Stone* that great artists need to maintain creative control and not do things just because it's so easy to take the money. Either you have the moral will to be firm about your art, or you're a sellout.

The trajectory of Alanis's body of work appears to contravene this binary where artistic integrity sits on one side and commercial gain sits on the other. "Wake Up" offers some information about the criteria for and the extent to which Alanis can be said to have sold out. The song highlights the dangers of taking the path of least resistance, while simultaneously acknowledging the failed coping mechanism of trying to obey, trying to raise one's hand politely: "And there's an underestimated and impatient little girl / Raising her hand // But it's easy not to / So much easier not to." If everyone is responsible for their own wokeness and no amount of our insistence to their sleepier selves can succeed in waking them up, we must naturally wonder where Alanis draws the line on compromise positions for herself.

Regarding "Wake Up," Alanis says in the Broadway musical book that "the little girl in here is me. The song is about the patriarchy and being on the receiving end of narcissism. The level of patronizing behavior I've received from men is ridiculous." She also says of the "you" addressed in the song, "Though I was only nineteen at the time I wrote this, I was speaking to all the men in my life." The question this begs is halfway to the joke's punchline: no female musician working in the 1990s can be said to have sold out because the price of their entry into the system was just so damn high that no amount of cash would be enough to justify it. Perhaps we can even remove the decade qualifier and make it an evergreen argument. Look no further than Taylor Swift, who has spent the 2020s rerecording her first six albums so that she can control the masters for them, hoping fans will stream the new versions and thus help her make up for all the money the original recordings funneled to Scooter Braun, the music producer who repeatedly bullied her.

While some artists or fans may oppose any compromise, others feel they need to be flexible lest they perish. When

Alanis was nineteen, she wrote "Wake Up." When Ani DiFranco was nineteen, she founded the iconic indie label Righteous Babe Records. As *JLP* came out in 1995, Ani was telling *Spin* that she started RBR because "I couldn't face having to compromise the things that I believe in and change the way that I work. And that's what a lot of people have to do when they're in the industry, is start to make compromises." Alanis echoed the same sentiment to *Rolling Stone* that same year: "The more you're willing to compromise, the more you're willing to go for the big bucks, the more you're willing to cut corners and sacrifice your creativity for financial gain. And that's just not something that's ever interested me."

Her exercise of good judgment in the manner she describes produces work that has not been met with the same awesome levels of acclaim as *JLP*. For example, the *So-Called Chaos* album, released in 2004, was labeled as "more accessible" as if this were an insult to Alanis's decision-making process about her own art. This is the only album whose title is the same as one of her song titles, rather than taken out of one of the verses. She is smiling on the album cover, learning to have more of a sense of humor about her work and not take it all as seriously as she used to back in the day. The theme of the album seems to be that every problem has a solution, that it'll all simply work out somehow. Especially in "So-Called Chaos," the idea is that the alleged chaotic nature of living an idle life turns out to be preferable to the well-organized and rigidly structured routines of a hardworking creative, the role in which she's always cast herself. The last track, "Everything," makes clear that she feels able to bring her whole self to the music these days because she has a partner who loves her despite all the challenges encountered as a result of partnership. *So-Called Chaos* was her first studio album not to debut at the top of the charts, although the video for "Everything" makes the case that her fans will stay with her despite any weak spots or failings in her latest work.

The "Eight Easy Steps" video also offers a good contrast between grown-up Alanis and the teenage Alanis of "Wake Up," depicting how her anger is now divided between self-loathing and societal hypocrisy, the system that set her up to fail in whatever ways she has. As the video rewinds further and deeper, through some of her past music videos that we covered in chapter 8 and back to her home movies as a baby, she recreates all the facial movements and the looks to make it seem as though she's been singing "Eight Easy Steps" all the way through these iconic moments in her life. The lyrical juxtapositioning and listings are close to exhibiting some of the same tensions as "Hand in My Pocket," with the idea that she can still rather campily mimic her bygone selves. All those faces and moments are still inside of her and can be deployed with the same youthful vigor, though now tempered by an adult sense of both stability and sarcasm. It's as if she used to question it all when she saw it for the first time, but now that she has seen it all, she's able to question herself just as much.

In a weird way, themes of resiliency showcased by her later work leave her open to accusations of selling out. Ironically, it's as if Alanis is seen as no longer angry enough for our contemporary taste and modernized marketplace. As musicologist and philosopher Robin James writes in *Resilience & Melancholy: Pop Music, Feminism, Neoliberalism*, "Sexism, then, is not a bug but a feature. Because it's not the sexism that needs collective overcoming, but individual women that need to be 'resilient' in the face of unavoidable, persistent sexism. This is not about overcoming patriarchy, but about upgrading it."

Alanis might answer for this more broadly in the same vein as her narrow address to *Q* magazine when *Supposed Former Infatuation Junkie* debuted in 1998. She said, "I knew that some people would feel like I sold out, and that's okay. I'm very clear that my work is not for everyone. But if I'm being true to myself, that's all I can do." James argues that even the feminist messages that are true to us can suffer from co-option. Anything resembling sincerity or authenticity on the model that we demanded in the nineties can be steered, these days, toward making a bunch of money. James again: "The corporate music industry now profits from subcultural sounds and aesthetics that used to evade and challenge it—what used to kill it now makes it stronger, as Nietzsche would say. Contemporary race/gender/sexuality politics are similarly upgraded."

Fears of the inevitable co-option inherent in all our creative outputs aside, we can ground ourselves in the question of what we intentionally allow. Alanis's lack of interest in selling out has been consistently demonstrated over the years. After her Canadian Walk of Fame induction in 2005, she reflected on the calibration of all her projects and posted a comment on the Walk of Fame website that her "life purpose is to inspire courage and compassion and the raising of consciousness on this planet so then every little thing that I do—whether it's a conversation I have or a relationship I nurture, a tour that I go on or a song that I write—serves me to see how in alignment it is with my purpose. My choices are a lot easier when I have my purpose to reference."

Compare that to her decision not to appear in the 2022 Rock Hall of Fame induction tribute to Carly Simon. According to music critic Jessica Hopper, as of 2023, only 61 of the Rock Hall's 719 inductees were women. That works out to 8.48 percent, or as Hopper pointedly tweeted, "it's FUCKING GRIM BRO when [you're] doing worse than women-artists-on-country radio numbers (10%) and women headliners at major music festivals (13%)." Hopper was addressing bros in general, but social media at large zeroed in on Jann Wenner, cofounder of *Rolling Stone* magazine and the Rock Hall, who was ousted from the Hall's board of directors for sexist comments just six months later. Alanis released a statement on social media about the decision to skip Simon's induction into the Hall that said, "I have spent decades in an industry that is rife with overarching anti-women sentiment and have tolerated a lot of condescension and disrespectfulness, reduction, dismissiveness, contract-breaching, unsupportiveness, exploitation and psychological violence (and more) throughout my career. [. . .] Thankfully, I am at a point in my life where there is no need for me to spend time in an environment that reduces women."

So, she is still talking back. Or, in James's terms, using "a method of correcting people who underestimate one's authority. The problem here isn't the Diva's—the person she's talking back to is the one who is dysfunctional and damaged. Talking back is, basically, saying, 'It's not me, it's you.' [. . .] Talking back feeds patriarchal damage back on itself, identifying patriarchy itself, not women, as the damaged thing that needs to be fixed." As the lyrics for "Wake Up" remind us, "There's no fundamental excuse for the granted I'm taken for" in these anti-woman situations.

Neoliberal capitalism ensures the profits, that "what goes around never comes around" in the form of consequences for patriarchs. The economic shift away from government regulation toward a truly free privatized and globalized market began way back in the seventies, but it surged through the Reagan era and had perhaps just reached the cusp of fully capturing the American imagination by the nineties. Individualism and competition were already key concepts guiding the music industry when *JLP* was released, but our picture is even clearer now in the throes of digital revolution, the internet, and the rise of artificial intelligence.

On the one hand, *JLP* can be viewed as a critique of neoliberalism. It expresses solid support for what we now think of as wokeness. In its affirmations of feminine empowerment, definitions of equal and balanced relationships, and consciousness-raising about mental health topics, *JLP* was a battle-ax on the front lines of the nineties culture wars. Alanis helped us to articulate the disillusionment we felt and taught us to cope with frustration about those insidious values that were hiding behind the mask of societal norms. The album helped stave off acquiescence to such pressures. On the other hand, it seems like an album that has sold thirty-three million copies worldwide to date probably has to be an instrument of the system to a certain extent. Anything that makes that much money must be inherently corrupted.

I no longer see in such starkly black and white terms as these, but as a teenager, I felt that selling out was a very "pass or fail" enterprise. This brings us back to something we touched on in chapter 5, the Riot Grrrl movement as a collective ontology that might be a successful hedge against the worst aspects of neoliberalism. Bikini Kill's Kathleen Hannah, the vocalist who fronted the pioneering riot grrrl band, told *Paper* magazine in 1998, "I've had people say to me, 'You guys would be really big if you lost a little weight and wore more makeup.' But the point of Bikini Kill was to be ugly, to be abrasive, to make people confront what they don't like." Alanis was using *JLP* to describe societal tensions and industry hassles, but the album and her self-presentation did not actually conform to the materialism and superficiality she described.

In hindsight, we can see how feminist anger and resistance themselves get co-opted by the music industry. Tori Amos told *Rolling Stone* in 1994, "I think our generation loves our pain, and if you dare fucking take it away from us, we're going to kill you. We like our pain. And we're packaging it, and we're selling it." Or we can again reach back to 1999 and Elizabeth Wurtzel, whose satisfyingly brash answer to the fear of co-option is neatly laid out in her book *Bitch*: "And if women want to engage in the legal system to forward freedoms or just because we're stark, raving, plumb-crazy mad and we're fed up and we want revenge, we've got to learn to collect the cash and laugh all the way to the bank or Barneys or the beach island paradise of our Rousseauvian dreams. We women need to learn to exact a pound of flesh by good, capitalist means."

Riot Grrrl is lauded for launching a thousand girl bands, but we should wonder how many of those bands survive today, how much those bands that did survive may have compromised to score a major label deal, and whether any of them have sold even 10 percent as many albums as Alanis has by now. But maybe these are the wrong standards by which to pass judgment on the success of any creative person or group. The past has funny ways of helping us out, often by letting us down. Kim France, a journalist at *Spin* magazine, asked Alanis about her lack of classic rock knowledge in all earnestness in 1999: "But what would [you] say to people who accuse [you] of not understanding rock—who say that you have to understand what came before you in order to be an artist?" To which Alanis replied, "I would say, 'Apparently not.'"

Seems like the same can be true of Girl Power pioneering. Critics say Alanis slipped across the thoroughly policed borders of the major label system to achieve superstardom by being nonthreatening in her feminism and stereotypical in her femininity, that she watered down the strategies needed for the mission. Those are matters of opinion, with which the bones in my body strongly disagree. I know what I felt at fifteen. Even if we appraise her work in as conservative and dismissive a neoliberal mode as possible, we still have to admit that it's a gateway drug. More authentically and to the point, *JLP* activated me as a revolutionary. I was a Midwestern kid whose radio only played the Top 40. I was an ancient twenty-two before I ever heard of Kathleen Hannah. If *JLP* represents a sanitized, diluted, or overly commercialized form of Girl Power, so be it. Alanis still did the trick, and here I am today.

13

WITHOUT PERMISSION

At the end of *Jagged Little Pill*, Alanis includes "Your House" as a hidden track. The secret bonus song is a minor rebellion against commercial music packaging that is as old as the Beatles, but hidden tracks really took off in tandem with the proliferation of compact discs. The CD format was popular by 1985 and outsold cassettes for the first time in 1989; then Apple introduced the first iPod in 2001 and that was the end of the CD. In the first half of the decade, even before Alanis was working on *JLP*, there were several extremely popular hidden tracks: in 1991, "Endless, Nameless" on Nirvana's *Nevermind*; in 1992, tracks by Nine Inch Nails and Dr. Dre; in 1993, a secret bonus track by alt rockers Cracker, along with tracks by Janet Jackson and Guns N Roses; and, in 1994, Green Day's *Dookie*. Then Alanis released "Your House."

The a cappella sparseness of it is a stunning contrast to the hard-rocking and thoroughly layered noisiness of the rest of the album. Its vast sonic emptiness is a bucket of cold water after listeners have been heated up by the full emotional range of the album. The song is hidden on the album just as the woman in the song is hidden in a man's house. She is trespassing there while he is absent, and I can't help but insert us, the audience, into her shoes, assuming a vantage point from which we may ask whether the project of this book has itself trespassed. After all, in her reflection on writing the *JLP* Broadway musical, Diablo Cody says in the musical book that the album "was a seismic event that shifted the plates of pop culture and redefined irony for a generation." Of her own hand in it, Cody reflects, "As I began the creative process in earnest, it dawned on me that writing the book for *Jagged Little Pill* was more than just a cool story to tell my friends or a retroactive treat for my teenage self—it was a tremendous responsibility."

Indeed, my hope is that this work has highlighted and preserved, rather than stepped on, any of the passionate sentience, psychic vulnerability, and emphatic contradiction that Alanis has always foregrounded in her music and her many other projects. This book can only begin to trace them, and there is no reason to offer any comprehensive conclusions about a creative person whose artistic output is still very much ongoing. "Your House" itself recommends moving slowly to soak everything in, treading lightly so as not to disturb the energy of the space, and yet studying deeply whatever or whoever has bewitched you. To remain interested only in *JLP* is like confining oneself to exploring only the kitchen, never entering the other spaces of the house, and therefore totally missing that there's a meditation room. As opposed to the shocking letdown of discovering someone else's love letter in "Your House," what we've discovered is that Alanis has been faithfully evolving the ideas of *JLP* all this time. The house *JLP* built has been renovated and we can recognize the bones of it everywhere when we turn toward the newer materials. May the roads we have taken to arrive at this understanding need no forgiveness.

After the miracle of *JLP*, something had to happen next. I had just turned seventeen and was preparing to graduate from high school, finally getting the hell out of town, when *Supposed Former Infatuation Junkie* came out. In whatever ways the album may have been a departure from her previous work, it was still undeniably Alanis due to its honesty, complexity, and deeply personal approach. Let's use the ideas of thanksgiving here to steer toward an overall sense of the responsibility we as fans of Alanis have to the musician and to her total body of work. The cover of *Junkie* is among my personal favorites because it really seems to encapsulate everything. It's a photo of Alanis's mouth, perhaps singing or speaking or laughing or smiling, her perfect white teeth and healthy gums all showing in front of her tongue, which is tensed for noisemaking. This image asks whether you think the glass is half empty or half full—whether this mouth is about to excoriate you, as on *JLP*; whether it's a middle finger to every exec who told her she needs to smile more; or whether it's genuinely light and joyful after her adventures in India.

The beautiful yet unsettling ambiguity of the cover photo is complicated by a textual overlay that lists a chunk of the Buddhist precepts she studied during her travels on the break after *JLP*: "We ask you to abide by the following moral code upon the premises. Please refrain from killing, stealing, lying, sexual misconduct, taking intoxicants, playing music, singing, please dress respectfully." Her teeth and tongue are poised for action while the text imposes a set of no-nonsense moral guidelines. It's a powerful evocation of the contradictions and challenges inherent in living a spiritual and meaningful life in this world.

To put a "no music" rule on an album cover is to promote the joy of trespass, to believe in the rule and to believe in breaking the rule simultaneously.

The list of rules in the text overlay is often incorrectly assumed to refer to the well-known "Five Precepts." In Buddhism as in other religions, there are varying intensity levels of practice: for example, you can be a layperson, a serious yogi, or a novice monk. Laypeople work with a list of five precepts that ends with a prohibition against taking intoxicants. Serious yogis work with eight precepts, which include a prohibition on entertainment like singing or dancing. The list on *Junkie* is missing the prohibition on eating after noon and on comfortable furniture, so it's seven rules instead of eight. Beyond this, novice monks would forgo using money. The list Alanis offers on the album cover is more than the path of the layperson but less than the path of a monk, and despite its strict tone, it's looser in its content due to missing a few prohibitions.

Perhaps she went to India seeking some means of plugging the holes she'd already found in Western philosophy and to aid her in navigating the perilous experience of being a superstar in a culture guided by such a philosophy, yet the music she made immediately afterward affords Eastern counterparts the same "both-and" critical approach that she gives to Catholicism on *JLP*. "Baba" issues a warning against guru capitalism and the self-help industry that runs parallel to the reflections in "Forgiven," even ending with some incantations of "Ave Maria." The driving rhythm and aggressive vocals of "Baba" create a sense of urgency and indignation, as Alanis rails against the false promises and hollow platitudes that are all too common in the market for self-improvement products.

Junkie reflects her critical embrace of both Eastern and Western philosophies as she seeks to find her own way in a world that often fails to meet her expectations. This is particularly evident in "Thank U" and "That I Would Be Good," which both offer a prayerful response to the existential challenges of life. Alanis is encouraging listeners to look beyond the material possessions and societal norms that often distract us from true fulfillment.

"Thank U" is a meditation on gratitude and humility, with lyrics that acknowledge humanistic struggle while also celebrating the beauty and wonder of our fallibility, of our merely mortal nature. The stripped-down arrangement and hypnotic melody create a sense of stillness and contemplation, inviting us as listeners to reflect on our own experiences and emotions. It's both global and personal, using a classic list structure to highlight the Westernized quick fixes that generally fail to address the deeper issues at hand. The song begins with a simple statement: "How 'bout getting off these antibiotics? How 'bout stopping eating when I'm full up?" It then adds many layers, incorporating a range of experiences and emotions, until at the end everything but the initial synth drops out, opening space for rumination as in "Your House," and in contrast to the anxiety-inducing pause that forecloses any thinking in "You Oughta Know."

The video for "Thank U" is equally powerful, iconically depicting Alanis wandering naked around Los Angeles. Her long hair covers her breasts, and the rest is a digital blur. Her vulnerable and unguarded state is a symbol of her willingness to be open to the world, even when it is chaotic and overwhelming. By imagining herself as a serene presence and calming force in an otherwise hectic world, she inhabits a space that is slowed down, making some communion with divinity actually possible. Her sense of peace and connection can be found even amid the painful and anarchic flow of life speeding by. "Thank U" is also a reflection on the nature of gratitude itself. The lyrics list examples of the things that Alanis is thankful for, including nothingness, terror, disillusionment, consequence, and frailty. By reframing the bad stuff within the bigger picture, she exhorts us to recognize that even our most difficult experiences are opportunities for expansion and metamorphosis.

Similarly, "That I Would Be Good" is a plea for acceptance and understanding, a reminder that in our darkest or weakest moments we are still worthy of love and compassion. The song's gentle acoustic guitar, flute work by Alanis herself, and soaring vocals create a sense of intimacy and vulnerability, as if she's singing directly to us, offering comfort and support. This prayer addresses the struggle to be human in a world that often judges us harshly. It is a benediction in response to the haters, the people who would classify us as bad for whatever reason. As Alanis says in a footnote in the musical book, "Every single line of this song is a deep prayer for me." She goes on to say that "this musical, and almost every song I write, is a prayer for the allowance to be human."

Junkie is full of reminders that our worth as a human being isn't determined by external achievement or the opinion of others, but by our innate dignity and value. That's a smart takeaway as a hedge against the stardom that followed the release of *JLP*, but it has also been her lifelong mission to assert those facts—that we can embrace our unique selves, speak out against injustice and oppression, and find hope and healing amid struggle. Despite letdowns along the way, Alanis has used her creative projects to grapple with spiritual and emotive complexity, exploring questions of identity, morality, and personal growth without getting bogged down in an existential dread of the inevitable contradictions.

From *JLP* onward, she doesn't offer easy answers or quick fixes, inviting us instead to join her on a journey of self-discovery and reflection that somehow always manages to steer back around to hope for growth and positive transformation. We have a responsibility to honor and respect her descriptions of this common quest when we use her work to fuel our own way forward in life, engaging thoughtfully with the nuances of her projects and treating them with care for her vulnerability in offering them up to us. In reflecting on *JLP* in the musical book two decades later, Alanis says, "For me, it is essentially a record about permission giving—the permission to feel anger, rage, sadness, grief, ambivalence, terror, numbness. It's about permission to fail, stand back up, and fall again—permission to be human."

That Alanis would be good if she were no longer queen has already proved out. That I would be good if I lost my youth has already proved out. We're both still kicking around just like back in the day, except more wisely or at least with a different flavor of foolishness. No more closures: I tried to close the book on Alanis after that first album, and thankfully, I failed—although I can hardly believe how long I took to realize it. I've needed permission to be human many more times than just that once, with that one album that got me through the second half of the nineties. Blessed be disillusionment.

ACKNOWLEDGMENTS

Thank you, Alanis.

Thank you, Mindy, my coheadliner on this lifelong tour.

Thank you to Karen Zarker, my editor at *PopMatters*; to Tanya Pearson, director of the Women of Rock Oral History Project; and to all the women and queers who worked in or are working in music, as artists or critics or behind the scenes or anything, regardless of how briefly or how small. We all matter.

And thank you to the good people at the University of Texas Press.

WORKS CONSULTED

Anderson, Steve, dir. *Fuck*. Mudflap Films/Rainstorm Entertainment, 2005.

Aron, Elaine N. *The Highly Sensitive Person: How to Thrive when the World Overwhelms You*. New York: Broadway Books, 2013.

Bakhtin, M. M. *Problems of Dostoevsky's Poetics*. Translated by Caryl Emerson. Minneapolis: University of Minnesota Press, 1984.

Barthes, Roland. *Elements of Semiology*. New York: Hill & Wang, 1967.

Barthes, Roland. *S/Z*. New York: Hill & Wang, 1974.

Berlant, Lauren. *Cruel Optimism*. Durham, NC: Duke University Press, 2011.

Berlant, Lauren. *Female Complaint: The Unfinished Business of Sentimentality in American Culture*. Durham, NC: Duke University Press, 2008.

Chaplin, Julia. "Jagged Little Pill: Why Alanis Morissette's Album Is Still Relevant 20 Years On." *The Guardian*, June 15, 2015. https://www.theguardian.com/lifeandstyle/womens-blog/2015/jun/15/jagged-little-pill-alanis-morissette-most-important-album-90s.

Cobain, Kurt. "Kurt Cobain: The Rolling Stone Interview." *Rolling Stone*, January 27, 1994, 54–65.

Cody, Diablo, Alanis Morissette, et al. *Jagged Little Pill*. New York: Grand Central Publishing, 2020.

Creney, Scott. "Ten '90s Albums More Feminist than Alanis Morissette's Jagged Little Pill." *Collapse Board*, November 12, 2013. http://collapseboard.com/ten-90s-albums-more-feminist-than-alanis-morissettes-jagged-little-pill/.

Crowe, Cameron, dir. *Say Anything*. Gracie Films, 1989.

DiFranco, Ani. "The Diva Next Door." *Spin*, March 1996, 78–83.

Dunn, Katherine. *On Cussing*. Brooklyn, NY, and Portland, OR: Tin House Books, 2019.

Fournier, Karen. *The Words and Music of Alanis Morissette*. Praeger Singer-Songwriter Collection. Santa Barbara, CA: Praeger Publishing, 2019.

France, Kim. "Ray of Light." *Spin*, April 1999, 97–104.

Friedman, Jaclyn. "My Humps, Her Irony: Alanis Morissette and the Transformation of a Gendered Text." *Women's Studies in Communication* 35, no. 2 (2012): 207–226. https://doi.org/10.1080/07491409.2012.691849.

Garland-Thomson, Rosemarie. *No Bad Parts: Healing Trauma and Restoring Wholeness with the Internal Family Systems Model*. Louisville, CO: Sounds True, 2022.

Hagood, Caroline. *Weird Girls*. New York: Bellevue Literary Press, 2021.

Hanna, Kathleen. "Don't Call Me Babe." *Paper* 19, no. 2 (October 1998): 56–61.

Heselgrave, Douglas. "The Ironic Cover Song and the Critique of the Postmodern Condition: Alanis Morissette's 'My Humps.'" *Popular Music and Society* 36, no. 1 (2013): 1-17. https://doi.org/10.1080/03007766.2012.715065.

Hiatt, Brian. "Alanis Morissette: Little Miss Perfect?" *Rolling Stone*, April 6, 1995, 38–45.

Hopper, Jess (@jesshopp). "Do they tho?" Twitter, March 10, 2023, 1:19 a.m. https://twitter.com/jesshopp/status/1634076591855681536.

Honig, Bonnie. *Antigone, Interrupted*. Cambridge: Cambridge University Press, 2013.

James, Robin. "Music Is Political: Introduction to the Symposium." *Journal of Popular Music Studies* 32, no. 4 (2020): 7–10.

James, Robin. "The Politics of Sonic Cyberfeminism." *The Oxford Handbook of Music and Virtuality*, edited by Sheila Whiteley and Shara Rambarran, 439–454. Oxford: Oxford University Press, 2016.

James, Robin. *Resilience and Melancholy: Pop Music, Feminism, Neoliberalism*. Zero Books, an imprint of Collective Ink, 2015.

James, Robin. *Sonic Episteme: Music, Literature, and Non-Expressive Sound*. Durham, NC: Duke University Press, 2019.

Klosterman, Chuck. *The Nineties*. London: Penguin Books, 2022.

Leigh, Wendy. *Modern Attachment Parenting: The Comprehensive Guide to Raising a Secure Child*. Rockridge Press, by Callisto Media, 2019.

Morissette, Alanis. "Alanis Unplugged." *Q*, October 1998, 84–90.

Morissette, Alanis. "Ask Alanis Morissette: I Wish My Girlfriend Didn't Smoke Pot." *The Guardian*, April 1, 2016. https://www.theguardian.com/lifeandstyle/2016/apr/01/ask-alanis-morissette-wish-girlfriend-didnt-smoke-pot.

Morissette, Alanis. "Ask Alanis Morissette: I Worry about My Grandchildren's Diet." *The Guardian*, June 3, 2016. https://www.theguardian.com/lifeandstyle/2016/jun/03/ask-alanis-morissette-grandchildren-diet.

Morissette, Wade. *Transformative Yoga: Five Keys to Unlocking Inner Bliss*. Vancouver, BC: Aquarian Publishing, 2016.

Mundy, Chris. "Interview with Tori Amos." *Rolling Stone*, November 1994 (special edition). http://www.yessaid.com/int/1994-11_Rolling_Stone.html.

Nobile, Drew. "Critical Sustainabilities: Music, Ecology, and Environmentalism in Recent Literature." *Music Theory Online* 28, no. 4

(2022). https://mtosmt.org/issues/mto.22.28.4/mto.22.28.4.nobile.html.

Robinson, Lisa. *Nobody Ever Asked Me about the Girls: Women, Music and Fame*. New York: Henry Holt and Company, 2020.

Schilt, Kristen. "'A Little Too Ironic': The Appropriation and Packaging of Riot Grrrl Politics by Mainstream Female Musicians." *Popular Music and Society* 26, no. 1 (2003): 5–16. https://www.tandfonline.com/doi/abs/10.1080/0300776032000076351.

Vineyard, Jennifer. "Alanis Morissette: The Silence Is Over." MTV News, January 31, 2002. https://www.mtv.com/bands/m/morissette_alanis/news_feature_011802.

Walsch, Neale Donald. *Conversations with Teens: Spiritual Laws for Today's World*. Newburyport, MA: Hampton Roads Publishing Company, 2001.

Weiss, Mark. "Urban Ritual: Wailing in Amerindian Brazil." *American Ethnologist* 10, no. 4 (1983): 712–734. https://www.sas.upenn.edu/~gurban/pdfs/Urban-Ritual_Wailing_in_Amerindian_Brazil.pdf.

Wurtzel, Elizabeth. *Bitch: In Praise of Difficult Women*. New York: Anchor Books, 1999.

Yarrow, Allison. *90s Bitch: Media, Culture, and the Failed Promise of Gender Equality*. New York: Harper, 2018.

Zimmerman, Jess. *Women and Other Monsters: Building a New Mythology*. Boston: Beacon Press, 2021.

Žižek, Slavoj. *Did Somebody Say Totalitarianism? Five Interventions in the (Mis) Use of a Notion*. London and New York: Verso Books, 2002.